Praise for THE RECEPTIONIST

"Literary Reality: No other memoir on the market today has half the charm, wit, or verbal dexterity of *The Receptionist* . . . Superb."

—*New York Journal of Books*

"[A] graceful memoir . . . Ultimately, it's not her sexual saga but her evocation of the *Mad Men* working environment that makes Groth's memoir interesting. *The Receptionist* vividly depicts a largely vanished Manhattan in which Ritz Crackers were the foundation of hors d'oeuvres, martinis were the mainstay of lunches, and pliable, overqualified women were stuck in lowly jobs forever."

—*The Washington Post*

"A literate, revelatory examination of self."

—*The Boston Globe*

"If you are a fan of *The New Yorker* and New York City history, you'll adore this fascinating book about Groth's experience at the magazine, where she started at the age of 19 in 1957 and remained until 1978. A lot can happen in 20 years, in life, in society, and in publishing."

—*The Atlantic Wire,* "Best Revisitation of a Cultural Icon" of 2012

"Written in lean, graceful prose that offers ample evidence of [Groth's] talent, the book is as much a window into the mythologized publication as it is a chronicle of one woman's self-discovery."

—*The New York Times*

"[Groth's] collected the sort of gossipy anecdotes that would have you hanging on her every word at a literary cocktail party."

—*Entertainment Weekly*

"For those of us desperate for a *Mad Men* fix, this memoir goes down like a gin and tonic on a hot day . . . While readers may find her stories about writers such as poet John Berryman or essayist Joseph Mitchell amusing, what interested me was Groth's depiction of those times, and how she reinvented herself while standing still." —*Chicago Tribune*

"An articulate, inviting book . . . That narrative, of an aspiring woman in a heady and male-dominated milieu, is compelling." —*The Seattle Times*

"An evocative memoir." —*People*

"Groth can be charmingly offhanded: anecdotal, gently gossipy . . . The Berryman chapter, one of the first in the book, is also among the finest . . . 'As a poet-teacher,' she recalls, 'he so invested his ego in his work that he was ego-free, a fleshless, selfless lover of enlightenment, pure spirit.' That's a terrific description, evoking not just his classroom style but also the humor and erudition of his poems." —*Los Angeles Times*

"Provide[s] fresh and memorable perspectives of the literati of the 1960s and 70s." —*The Louisville Courier-Journal*

"[A] lovingly crafted memoir." —*Daily Candy*

"Intimate and breezily conversational . . . A woman's story of her own becoming amid the chaos and glitz of Manhattan in the 1960s."
—*Shelf Awareness*

"Groth . . . isn't a woman to give up, and by the end of the book, she finds her own delightful voice, which is the book's real pleasure."
—Oprah.com

"A rare take on pre-liberation office life told from the distaff side . . . An intoxicating look inside the *New Yorker.*"

—*The Local,* a *New York Times* Blog

"[Groth] paints a picture of a naive Midwesterner with a mane of thick blond hair coming of age in the 1960s and 1970s, experiencing the era's turbulent politics and sexual revolution, all from behind the receptionist desk."

—The Associated Press

"Are you a *New Yorker* magazine groupie? Do you wait every week just to laugh at the cartoons and read Talk of the Town? If so, we have a book for you . . . The magazine's eccentricity was not lost on Groth. Lucky for us."

—Craig Wilson, *USA Today*

"[A] graceful memoir."

—*Mother Jones*

"I truly loved this book . . . Ms. Groth provides sharp and very personal insight into some of the greatest writers of the last century, as well as a fascinating look inside the magazine that has shaped American culture like no other. But she also provides something very different, but equally transfixing: The poignant narrative of her own coming of age, as a woman, a writer, and a thinker—and, ultimately, the sort of wry iconoclast who would produce this lovely, moving, and utterly engrossing book."

—Joanna Smith Rakoff, author of *A Fortunate Age*

"One of the most buzzed-about memoirs of the summer . . . *The Receptionist* is a don't-miss memoir of an era, a literary magazine and a fascinating woman."

—SheKnows.com

"What a superb book. Beautifully written, so very frank, and with many insights into the world of magazine publishing. I can see a film, in the tradition of the one based on Rona Jaffe's *The Best of Everything*."

—Foster Hirsch, author of *The Dark Side of the Screen*

"[Groth] is witty, honest, and self-deprecating, without whining, and quite a good role model." —*Booklist*

"Revelatory . . . Deeply reflective . . . Groth chronicles the many dazzling personalities whose lives touched, and moved, hers." —*Publishers Weekly*

"An honest and engaging memoir for fans of the magazine and histories of *Mad Men*–era New York." —*Library Journal*

"A nostalgic, wistful look at life inside one of America's most storied magazines, and the personal and professional limbo of the woman who answered the phone . . . This bookish girl from flyover country who became a *Mad Men*–era hottie, and who found she had to leave this cozy nest in order to save herself, is very much an interesting character in her own right. For readers who can't get enough *New Yorker* lore, an amiable view from the inside." —*Kirkus Reviews*

"With her piled-up blonde hairdo bent over the telephone messages she wrote by hand, Groth served for years in an aquarium-like booth as gatekeeper for a talented, tight-knit, rapscallion community. In this evocative memoir she is exuberantly frank about her young self, fresh from the corn belt, discovering sex and the city through two vanished worlds: *The New Yorker* of editor William Shawn and bohemian Greenwich Village."

—Kennedy Fraser, former *New Yorker* writer and author of *Ornament and Silence: Essays on Women's Lives*

The Receptionist

THE RECEPTIONIST

An Education at *The New Yorker*

JANET GROTH

ALGONQUIN BOOKS OF CHAPEL HILL | 2013

Published by
Algonquin Books of Chapel Hill
Post Office Box 2225
Chapel Hill, North Carolina 27515-2225

a division of
Workman Publishing
225 Varick Street
New York, New York 10014

First paperback edition, Algonquin Books of Chapel Hill, June 2013.
Originally published by Algonquin Books of Chapel Hill in 2012.
Printed in the United States of America.
Published simultaneouly in Canada by
Thomas Allen & Son Limited.
Design by April Leidig.

The following were first published elsewhere in slightly different form:
"Homage to Mister Berryman" appeared in the *New England Review*,
Volume 29, Number 3, 2008. It was nominated for a Pushcart Prize
and won honorable mention in the Pushcart Prize volume, 2008.

"Lunching with Joe" appeared in *Southwest Review*,
Volume 93, Number 4, 2008.

Library of Congress Cataloging-in-Publication Data
Groth, Janet, [date]
The receptionist : an education on the eighteenth floor /
Janet Groth.—1st ed.
p. cm.
ISBN 978-1-61620-131-9 (HC)
1. Groth, Janet, [date] 2. New Yorker (New York, N.Y. : 1925)—
Biography. 3. Periodicals—Publishing—New York (State)—New York—
History—20th century. 4. Receptionists—Biography. I. Title.
PN4900.N35G76 2012
051—dc23

[B] 2012003336

ISBN 978-1-61620-306-1 (PB)

10 9 8 7 6 5 4 3 2

KEVIN WALLACE

Janet Groth in 1962.

Contents

The Receptionist

Introduction; or, Jack Spills the Beans

It all happened by the merest chance. Or perhaps the heavens *were* aligned. In August 1957 I finished my BA degree at the University of Minnesota. At the same time I received a phone call telling me of some upcoming excitement in the area—a manned balloon flight into the stratosphere was being filmed for a CBS science show. Thinking that it would advance my dream of seeking fame and fortune as a writer, I managed to secure a temporary job as assistant to Arthur Zegart, the show's writer-director. It went well, and Mr. Zegart invited me to send him a copy of my résumé should I decide to come to New York. He received it three weeks later while fishing in Maine with his friend E. B. White and promptly arranged an interview for me when Mr. White returned to his office at *The New Yorker.*

E. B. White was then one of the best-known writers on the magazine, but his shyness, I found out later, was of mythic proportions, and this interview quite unprecedented. He seemed pained to be in the presence of anyone at all, much less a corn-fed girl from Iowa who was looking for a job.

"What sort of work do you envision doing, Miss Groth?" His

handsome, fine-featured gray head was lowered, his eyes cast down, his voice little above a whisper. I was overwhelmed with a desire to put the poor man at ease.

"Well, I want eventually to write, of course, but I would be glad to do anything in the publishing field."

Mr. White took a moment to absorb this information. When he could bring himself to speak again, he asked, "Can you type?"

"Not at a professional level," I said.

He coughed and looked at the résumé that Arthur Zegart had given him and that had led to my being there in his office. "What about this short story prize you won? This Anna Augusta Von Helmholtz Phelan prize," he said. "Was that story typed?"

I told him that yes, of course it had been, but that I deliberately maintained a slow, self-devised system that involved looking at the keyboard.

"I was afraid, you see, that if I became a skilled typist, I would wind up in an office typing pool."

For the first time Mr. White looked directly at me. "And you don't want to wind up there?" he asked.

I suspected that he had some sympathy for the course I had taken.

"No, I think anything would be more interesting to me than that," I said. How rash and how fateful that course turned out to be!

After a few more questions, Mr. White concluded the interview by calling into his office Miss Daise Terry. I later found out she was a formidable figure around the magazine, its manager in charge of secretarial personnel. A petite woman of four feet nine or ten, no more than five feet, even in inch-and-a-half heels, she had a cap of tightly curled white hair and a slash of geranium-pink lipstick in a face dominated by piercing blue eyes. At perhaps sixty or so, she needed no glasses.

Handing her my résumé, White said, "Miss Groth is looking for a job here at the magazine but would rather not be in the typing pool. Will you see if there is anything you can do for her?"

"I will," she said, asking me to come with her.

I learned that she, too, was from the middle of the country, having left her native Kansas in 1918 to join the International Red Cross, and had wound up in New York after some years serving in Vienna.

She said, "Now, as a midwesterner, you have better sense than the Westchester County and Connecticut girls who come through this office. I always have to take them in hand and give them a stern talking-to about their behavior and conduct. We want ladylike clothing and ladylike behavior at all times."

She cast her eyes over my black linen dress and black pumps. "I see I needn't tell you that. I always think the best place to shop for the kind of thing we like to see is at Peck and Peck."

I said I would keep that in mind.

"At the moment," she said, "we have an opening at the reception desk down on eighteen—that's the writers' floor. There is not much traffic there, but the editor or two and the half-dozen writers whose offices are down there need someone to look after their mail and messages. Do you think that would appeal to you?"

I said that sounded fine.

"Good," she said. "You may report in to me for work on Monday morning at ten."

We shook hands, and I was officially a member of the editorial staff.

So that is how I got my "in" at *The New Yorker*—as they always say, it's not who you are but who you know. And so far, my story was typical, if a good deal luckier than most. There was every reason to suppose that if I didn't leave to marry, in the course of a year or two I would be joining the trail of countless trainees before me, moving either into the checking department or to a job as a Talk of the Town reporter, and perhaps from one of those positions to the most coveted of spots, that of a regular contributor with a drawing account.

Yet with the exception of one six-month stint in the art department, I did not rise from my initial post. The William Shawn years at *The New Yorker*, 1952–87, completely encompass my twenty-one years' employment there, from 1957 to 1978. I entered the workforce before the feminist era, and as I ponder the way women in general failed to thrive in that world, how often they were used and overlooked, I recognize that I was part of a larger historical narrative. As for my personal struggles, during much of the time in question, I was undergoing a prolonged identity crisis, and the real struggle, for me, was the one that arose from my proximity to all the creative people I served. Was I or was I not "one of them"? And since I didn't know, it is scarcely surprising that *The New Yorker* didn't know, either, what in the world to do with me.

I THOUGHT OF THE forty or so idiosyncratic inhabitants of the eighteenth floor as "my writers" and the six or so cartoonists billeted there as "my artists." I watered their plants, walked their dogs, boarded their cats, sat their children—and sometimes their houses—when they went away. Of course, I also took their messages. Not required in the skill set, but over the years I *received* messages, too, along with impressions, confidences, and an education in a variety of subjects. I was there, among the men and women who wrote and edited the magazine, for longer than many of them were. I watched their comings and goings, their marriages and divorces, their scandalous affairs, their failures and triumphs and tragedies and suicides and illnesses and deaths.

After leaving the magazine, I used various tactics to mask the lateral trajectory of my stay there. It was Jack Kahn (E. J. Kahn Jr., as he signed his *New Yorker* pieces) who blew my cover, all unintentionally. I'm sure he never guessed that I had been trying to keep a lid on my failure to advance at the magazine, imagining that I could hide it from the world at large as my own guilty secret.

In 1976 I taught a course at Vassar called The Contemporary Press. Jack was one of the writers from "my floor" who came up to Poughkeepsie as a guest speaker. He mentioned the event in his 1979 memoir *About the New Yorker and Me* and introduced me this way:

> In many respects, *The New Yorker* belies its reputation for institutional eccentricity. We have some writers and editors around who could pass for bankers and who, as they walk toward the New York Yacht Club on West Forty-fourth Street, could not unreasonably be expected by passersby to continue on inside. And yet we do have our authentic oddities. Jan Groth is surely one. She is finishing her Ph.D. dissertation in English. She has taught that subject at a high academic level. (She also writes an elegant Italian script.) But in twenty years or so she has never risen at the magazine—possibly of her own volition, though I doubt it—beyond being the eighteenth-floor

> receptionist, which is where she started off. We who spend many daylight hours there, mind you, are delighted with her permanence. She takes our messages when we are away from our desks, as we often are; she has learned to recognize the voices of our wives and children. As in our absences she comforts our friends, so when the occasion demands does she protect us against our enemies.

I am not sure what Jack meant by his reference to protecting him and the other writers from their enemies, but I can guess. He was endorsing my efforts to shield them from all distractions that would interfere with their work. I have more trouble with Jack's reference to me as one of *The New Yorker*'s "authentic oddities." It's one thing to joke to my fellow Lutherans about being an oddity as a churchgoer in a club full of secular humanists. It is quite another to find myself among *New Yorker* staffers who have been so characterized in *New Yorker* lore. There was, for example, the brilliant fact checker Dorothy Dean, who gave off manic vibes so electric they created a people-free zone of a ten-foot radius wherever she went. There was the magazine's Odd Couple (one of several such), this one consisting of shambling, grumpy Frederick "Freddie" Packard, also a fact checker, and his spouse, the publication's crackerjack grammarian Eleanor Gould. Miss Gould, a walking version of Fowler's *Modern English Usage,* would rank high in any listing of authentic oddities, and among our numerous hypochondriacs, Freddie outcomplained a roster of champs in that department. His best moment may have come when he famously began his reply to a colleague's routine inquiry into his health with "Well, I've got these two colds . . ." Freddie would have felt vindicated by a recent piece in Science Times declaring it perfectly possible to have two colds—a head cold and a sinus cold—simultaneously.

Others with colorful, weird propensities included the editor Rogers "Popsy" Whitaker—who, despite a perpetual frown, a thrust-forward lower lip, sagging suspenders, and a portly form, was inclined to pitch rose-laden woo at spoken-for damsels on the editorial staff—and the writers Maeve Brennan and St. Clair McKelway. Miss Brennan and Mr. McKelway were once young marrieds down in the Village but in their later years, split from each other, shared histories of colorful breakdowns. Miss Brennan, hoping to add height to her tiny frame, teased her red hair into a five-inch beehive, which, in her bouts of lost perspective, turned into a terrifying tangle as she forgot to give it the occasional brush. Mr. McKelway went in for crayoning the office walls periodically with shocking signs and logos that necessitated early morning scrubbings-down. The list could go on and on and include the overcoat-clad, claustrophobic editor in chief, Mr. Shawn himself. I have always loved the idea that *The New Yorker* was a place with broad limits of tolerance for unusual looks and behavior, a haven for the "congenitally unemployable," as Rogers Whitaker and A. J. Liebling are both reported to have said, but I had never thought of myself as belonging among them.

Certainly in the beginning I fit the normal profile, being one of the thousands who come to the city from the provinces and, according to E. B. White, give New York its dynamism and buzz. In *Here Is New York* he divides residents into three types. The first are the native born, the second the commuters, and the third—the source of the city's vitality, élan, and magical "deportment"—are those who come to it from the hinterland, the ones for whom the city is their destination, "the goal." I came as one of the third type.

What happened after I got there is a more complicated story.

Homage to Mr. Berryman

For a brief period in 1960 when he was in New York on academic vacation, the poet John Berryman was of the opinion that I would make him a good wife. He proposed this to me regularly. It seems he was, in the years between his second and third marriages, proposing to every halfway decent-looking woman he met. It was perhaps his way of acknowledging guilt at the failure of his previous marriages and an indication of his good intention to do better next time. Late in the sixties, at a women's group, he came up when the issue of male commitment arose—as an example of overcorrection. Among the seven women in the room, it turned out that he had proposed to three of us. And that was only in New York, in his spare time. The campuses where he taught in those bachelor years, 1959–61, were checkered with other potential Mrs. Berrymans. So it was perhaps not the mark of distinction it seemed in the moment.

John Berryman came into my life in 1956 as my teacher at the University of Minnesota. He was then a clean-shaven professor of humanities, teaching the classics from the Greeks to Shakespeare. Once exposed to his electrifying classroom technique, I took every class he offered. Then, once he'd begun to recognize me, after two or three semesters, I tagged along when he invited the best and the brightest of his students out for coffee and further discussion after class. Brilliant Jerry Downs was trained by the Jesuits, and troubled. I was bright enough to sit next to him, share notes—and Berryman. Jerry adored him, too, and when lucky enough to be asked, we would sit with him in some campus greasy spoon for an hour after class, or as long as Berryman's cigarettes held out. There, in a haze of smoke, Mr. Berryman, as we called him, held forth with ideas about everything from the text we were reading to his days at Clare College, Cambridge. He harbored nostalgic yearnings for those ivied halls, snowbound as he was in the wild terrain of northern Middle America.

A couple of years after my graduation, he reentered my life in his capacity as poet. On one of his visits to the office of Louise Bogan, the poetry editor of *The New Yorker,* he discovered me behind a desk on the editorial floor. Invitations to lunches and dinners ensued.

He had a personal triangle of stopping places when he was in Manhattan, from the Chelsea Hotel, to Chumley's on Bedford Street, to the White Horse on Hudson. My apartment was on Jane Street and so formed an insert in the baseline of his larger configuration. He would stop by, shouting his newest Henry poem, more pleased by it, more acute about its merits, chagrined about its weak lines, and acute about those, too, than any outside commentator could be.

His courting was full of high-flown compliments about the magnificence of my face, the golden flamingness of my hair, the metamorphosis of my body from its former student shape into what he perceived as its present womanly glories. But these remarks had a professorial, ex cathedra air about them. The real text of his conversation was more likely to be concerned with what he was writing, where he was reading his poems, how he was faring on one of his projects or another, or, with lapses into intimacy, something that his son—on a postdivorce visit—might have said to him as he watched his father shave. Berryman's talk was fast and compounded of so many diverse elements that ran into each other at such dizzying speed that I found it impossible to react. I felt vaguely stunned in his presence.

He never touched me except to draw his stretched-out second finger down the side of my face. I saw little of him, far too little to have justified his conviction that I would make him a good wife. There was only the occasional visit with a new poem and heavy compliments, or a telephoned summons to meet him at one of the points on his triangle, where there were sure to be others present. Youngsters, out on a date, hugged themselves and their beer mugs with delight at having stumbled on an evening with an authentic genius—eccentric, a poet, and in his cups.

So we made the rounds, or rather the angles, John dropping the great names of his famous friends, Cal and Saul and Delmore, and, when he was at the White Horse Tavern, of Dylan Thomas, another poet who drank more than was good for him. I sensed that he was both hurt and angry that he was not included in the ranks of those great and famous friends, had not achieved more, been recognized more. I knew, too, that he was hoping for the offer of a chair at Columbia—with what encouragement I am not sure, but he spoke of it as the hinge on which to swing our marriage. It did not seem to be forthcoming. I could not have married him anyway, for I was in love with somebody else. But it was clear that John was going through a bad time, and the time never seemed right for me to tell him that.

When I managed a diplomatic refusal, he went back to Minnesota. In the following year he married a young woman from Saint Paul called Kate. I became a person he looked up when he came into town from his many travels, to India and Dublin and elsewhere. Kate waited at home in Minnesota with a new baby and hopes of his recovery from alcoholism. He would call asking me to meet him somewhere, and I would arrive, only to discover that in the interim he had moved on. I might or might not go after him. If I did not, I would be treated to an early-hour rousting out of bed to find a weary cab driver supporting him on my doorstep. He had remembered, with sorrow, our broken date. I might get him to take a little coffee or tea as he sagged on my living room couch, smoking French cigarettes. He would not hear of sleep, not even when he was unfit for conversation. What helped was music. Certain Mozart quartets or any of the Brandenburgs commanded his reverent attention even when he could not speak.

The last time I saw John he was bearded and very famous indeed, having won a Pulitzer for *77 Dream Songs.* He, drunk and shirtsleeved and rambling; his publisher, Robert Giroux, sober and correct and embarrassed; and I, also sober, also correct, also embarrassed, met, supposedly to lunch, at Giroux's apartment on the Upper East Side. John came to the door bearing a water tumbler of bourbon in his trembling hand. Beads of cold sweat stood out on his forehead. Bob Giroux and I bounced worried suggestions off him about food and doctors, rest and warm baths. He would not hear a word from either of us. His talk was difficult to follow but brilliant. Among other, more personal comments about how fine I was looking and what sort of terms he hoped to get for his next book, he delivered a tercentenary tribute to Jonathan Swift and told us about a visit he had paid when he was a student at Clare College to the aged and oh-so-awe-inspiring Yeats, at which, as John recalled it, he tried to one-up Yeats. Then he shouted a few poems at us. Then, out nearly cold on the sofa, he made heartrending reference to what he knew he was doing, couldn't seem to stop himself from doing, to his wife—whose temporary retreat to New England with their child he applauded as "awfully wise." This outburst was followed by the emotionless invocation, "Please, God, let me be dead soon." It seemed as if he might at least sleep.

But his stick-thin frame was shaken upright again by the ringing of the doorbell. Lunch arrived. He began again on the bourbon and cigarettes. Would not take hold of a morsel of bread, much less a bite of a sandwich. I could not conceive that he could give a public reading that night. Yet at 8:00 p.m., I sat in the third row at the Guggenheim, next to Jane Howard, who was to write about him for *Life,* amid several hundred New York literati, and saw him do it. He was shaky, but he was eloquent, and his weaving and slurred speech only seemed to add to the drama and interest of the occasion.

Then one day I opened the newspaper to discover a photo of the bearded Berryman. Like everyone else in the literary world, I was shocked to read that on January 7, 1972, John had left his home, walked to the bridge that crossed the Mississippi on the left side of the Minneapolis campus, and jumped. I imagined him briefly looking down at the river as a block of ice floated by, waving to a young couple kissing on the campus-side bank. Whether he performed either of those actions, he did jump a hundred feet to his death, a pocket of his overcoat yielding only one document, a blank check.

We who used to fill to capacity the auditoriums of the universities and museums in which he read met once more at the Donnell Library for a memorial service. Poet friends read, but John stole the show. His familiar voice—on tape—made what had been a solemn and bleak occasion rocket toward hysteria with its power to evoke in us a mixture of laughter and grief.

In the years after his death, as I heard a sardonic Frenchman put it, "the dissertation bells went off all over the country." I hated it when I heard the way he was being talked of by junior professors at Modern Language Association conventions and reedy-voiced sophomores in poetry coffeehouses—expounding on his death wish, lumping him together with three or four others who happened, like him, to be dead by their own hand.

I found that those who had known him wrote or told about it as if the frazzled, badly behaved neuroses were *him*. How unjust! To me his value lay neither in the titillating gossip of his riotous life nor in the private gratification of having been admired by him. It is not the poems he left behind, though the poems loom large. It is the poet sage.

Since I could not watch John make his poems, the next best thing was to watch him teach. As a poet-teacher he so invested his ego in his work that he was ego-free, a fleshless, selfless lover and sharer of enlightenment, pure spirit. This part of him is neither personal nor notorious nor recorded anywhere at all except in his poems and in the memories of his students, where he exists as the chief item in the little library of hours we've brought away from our lives in the university.

For those of us who took his humanities course, this meant fifty minutes a day, five days a week, for five trimester terms. The course, called something like Western Civ, covered everything from the Greeks and Romans to Flaubert. As he taught it, it became a remarkable monument to the life of the mind—or whatever real education had better be called, now that to call it education is to give it a bad name.

He came in a little late, but faithfully. They say now that he was often hung over, or on ambulatory leave from some local drying-out clinic or halfway house or mental ward. Perhaps the latter were only facets of the later years of his tenure. I recall his missing only one class in the one and a half years I attended the course. The occasion must have been more serious and predictable than a spate of illness; when he was merely ill, he came. On that one day, he had arranged for a substitute chosen to make up to us for his absence—and perhaps in the case of anybody else's absence, it would have done.

He sent us his friend Saul Bellow, a visiting professor from Chicago, a figure who should have delighted our glamour-loving selves. Yet the one who came in John's stead struck us as dull stuff, a burned-out case to the likes of us, who had been fed on real flames of a real spirit. The day passed. Back came our man, passing the light and culture of the past through the shining honeycomb of his passionate personality, informing it with life and intelligence. With him we entered once more into the world of sacrifice and ritual, of meaning and conflict and beauty. Existential truth emerged and took on life and breath before us.

The more I hear this man reduced to the wasteful contours of a faintly ridiculous fame as one of the "confessional poets," the more necessary it seems to proclaim his real worth as manifested in his classroom.

He was, as I said, usually a few minutes late—a deliberate design on his part. There were no chummy huddles with the prof up front broken up by the bell, no fidgeting at the blackboard while stragglers got to their seats. He got straight to the business at hand. There was a sense of ceremony in his greeting—"Good afternoon, ladies and gentlemen"—and in the way he set his bulging briefcase down on a chair beside the front desk, opened it, and extracted the text of the day. He'd lay it on the desktop and walk to the windows that ran along the right side of the room (his right, our left), twisting the cord of the window shade into spirals as he began the discussion.

It never became clear why he brought the books that caused the bulge, since he referred only to the text at hand, and to his notes, if he brought any, not at all. Still, it was functional in a way, an outward and visible sign of all the background material he had gone through that now stood bulwark-like behind the easy command he displayed of his subject.

There was no talking down. If, in the course of opening a book, he paused to give us a disquisition on the correct way to open books, it was never with an air of condescension. Rather, he managed to convey the idea that there was always a best way to do even the simplest things, and to credit us with wanting to know that best way.

He began by pressing a few pages in from the back, opening flat, smoothing; pressing a few pages in from the front, opening flat, smoothing; then from the back a few, then the front, and so on, a few pages at a time, until he could lay the book open flat from the middle without breaking its spine.

In the same spirit of making us his confreres in technical inquiry, he took us into his confidence regarding his choice of which translation of a given classic we would be using. He went far beyond the point where any of us could hope to follow him in his comparison of the merits of the Rieu versus the Lattimore version of the *Iliad,* for example, or the Cohen versus the Putnam translation of *Don Quixote.* What did come through to us was the sense of what a tricky, delicate, and complicated thing it was to transfer poetic expression from one language to another. He showed a regard for our pocketbooks, too, assigning works in paperback, or, if he assigned hardcover books, seeing to it that the campus bookstores were stocked with inexpensive used copies.

He'd give us sample passages from rival translations whenever another version seemed to have an edge over the one we were using. But however good he thought the translation he had settled on, he never let us forget that we were getting only a fraction of the power inhering to the original. He read aloud to us in the original so that we might not altogether miss the aural contours of a work. This method made a vivid impression on me in two instances in particular. One, in a term dominated by Dante's *Inferno,* came in the Paolo and Francesca episode.

We were using the Ciardi translation, but we had samples of Longfellow, Sayers, and others as well. We were also grounded in the nature of the sin for which this pair of innocents had been condemned to circle through the whirlwind entwined in one another's arms. He put it to us that in Renaissance Italy, romantic love was downright seditious, an act of wanton rebellion on the part of marriageable children. Noble parents engaged in delicate negotiations to secure the perpetuation and, if possible, enlargement of their properties through marriage.

In such an environment the reading of any book of romance—certainly the book of Lancelot—in the company of a member of the opposite sex was flagrant disobedience. It was a reckless thing to do, never mind Francesca's disclaimer, as we first met it in Ciardi's notes: "We were alone, suspecting nothing." Even those of us who knew no Italian gained a greater sense of poignancy from the original, "Soli eravamo e sanza alcun suspetto." Though I suppose it would require the timbre of his voice as he read it to convey the full pressure of Berryman's feeling for these lines.

The second instance was a line of Hebrew from the poem of Job that knocked us out. By the time we got to it we were already veterans of the historical-critical method of biblical study practiced by Bultmann and others. We were aware of the folk origin of the beginning and end of the book of Job—the story of Job's initial state of happiness and the last images of how, after his tribulations, God restores everything he has lost and doubles it. We knew that these "frame narratives" were most probably added later than the core poem, which was the work of one "maker."

We plunge immediately into the opening lines of the authenticated poem, noting the progressive intensity with which Job calls down oblivion upon himself. The earliest stage of erasure is relatively impersonal: "Let the day perish wherein I was born," et cetera. But see the fanaticism of his curses, the successive degrees by which he seeks to expunge his own existence. He will call back, first, the day and the night in historical time of his birth, then the calendar dates, then the weather, the light, the meteorological and chronological particulars—all expunged in the specifics of the curses he hurls forth. Finally, Berryman tells us, the poet builds his poem in the Hebrew to a crescendo of outraged horror and revulsion over the moment of his conception, a cry so inadequate to the resources of

English that the language cannot do it justice: "The night in which it is said, There is a man child conceived . . . That night, let thick darkness seize upon it; let it not be joined unto the days of the year, let it not come into the number of the months. Lo, let that night be barren; let no joyful cry be heard in it . . . Let the stars of its dawn be dark; let it hope for light, but have none, nor see the eyelids of the morning; because it did not shut the doors of my mother's womb, nor hide trouble from my eyes."

"Listen," said Berryman, "and you shall hear the cry of a woman in sexual climax RENDERED INTO WORDS!"

We heard it. We who had never heard such a sound coming out of our own mouths—or the mouths of anyone we knew. We heard it, right there in room 123 of Johnston Hall.

To see and hear Berryman lecture on a text he loved was to be in the presence of the transcendent. To describe it otherwise would be imprecise—and he was ever one for precision.

On Writing, Not Writing, and Lunching with Joe

Although he said he doubted it, Jack Kahn posited my twenty-year employment flatline as my own eccentric choice. Closer to the truth than you knew, Jack. The choosing was all unconscious, however, so how much "choice" entered into it?

The dream I had of being a writer, a dream I carried with me to *The New Yorker*, began in my teens with the conviction that I was meant to be one. I had long harbored these yearnings—inevitable, I suppose, since I had spent many adolescent hours immersed in novels about the artist as a young man. (The gender switch was made easily enough; these were fantasies, after all.) I even wrote and submitted an entry to *Mademoiselle*'s short story contest. More of a teen angst reverie than a story, really, called "Night Thoughts," it featured the ineffable sense of loss that swept over the night thinker when a car's headlights moved from one corner of the bedroom ceiling to another and was gone. I didn't win that contest. Another blond with daddy problems won that year. Name of Sylvia Plath.

The dream went with me when I left home in September 1954. I started my adult life as a scholarship student living in a large Victorian house on the edge of the University of Minnesota campus. It was called, quaintly enough, Mrs. Smith's Tea Room. The scholarship covered books and tuition, the job at Mrs. Smith's covered room and board, and Mom and Dad sent three dollars a week pocket money. My gig was cutting pies into difficult-to-calculate numbers of equal pieces—Mrs. Smith wanted seven slices out of the six-slice tins and nine out of the eight. A wonderful Kerouac look-alike whose name, miraculously, was Jack, liked to josh with me while he waited to pick up the desserts and serve them at his tables—full of adoring girls—in the front dining room.

On my own at last, I found I need no longer be lonely. Suddenly I was among other people who liked to read. In the back room, tables full of graduate students—most of them male, with interesting, scruffy clothes and brooding looks—conducted passionate discussions about Miguel de Unamuno and Wallace Stevens within earshot of my pantry. I learned to smoke. I tried to look sophisticated in a blond chignon and mascara-darkened lashes and bought a trench coat—the first of a long line of trench coats—with epaulets! I was in heaven.

Exempt from freshman English, I took a creative writing course, turning my adolescent traumas into short stories. My writing teacher, Morgan Blum, a frog-like man from a place he called "Looz-iana," sat hunched over his desk in front of the beat-up lecture room in Folwell Hall, making me appreciate things like literary flashbacks, use of dialect, the Southern grotesque, and such. Professor Blum was especially well suited for Katherine Anne Porter and Faulkner, whose "A Rose for Miss Emily" he brought to vivid life. Several of the stories I wrote for him appeared, along with some poems I wrote for another course, in the campus literary magazine called the *Ivory Tower.*

All seemed to be going smoothly until I discovered a near-pathological shyness in myself. In the writing classes I took, student work was regularly read for discussion. I soon realized that I suffered inordinately whenever attention was called to my writing. It mattered not that it was favorable attention. This nervousness rose to near trauma at a literary evening held at the Pillsbury Mansion that winter. I knew it would be attended by Allen Tate, a star of the English faculty and a major American poet. His "Ode to the Confederate Dead" was in all the anthologies. In anticipation of having to read one of my stories aloud in front of him and the assembled company, I developed a migraine so severe that I asked the hostess to show me the nearest bathroom in which to be sick. She did, and afterward, with great understanding, she helped me to a darkened room. There she insisted I lie down on her own bed and pressed a damp washcloth to my brow, assuring me that someone else would read the story in my stead.

By the time sherry and biscuits were served following the readings, I was well enough to join the others. I was introduced to Professor Tate as the author of a story he'd heard earlier in the evening. I muttered something about wanting to tell him how much I liked his class in English poetry, but stammered that I was "having trouble verbalizing it." He looked kindly into my face and said in the deep and mellifluous voice with which he mesmerized his classes, "My dear child, that is *not* your difficulty." Such encouragement only seemed to worsen my self-consciousness. I went home in a state of helpless mal de mer, though the only water, the Mississippi River, was blocks away.

Crowning the paroxysms of self-doubt that accompanied each

distinction bestowed upon my work was the Delta Phi Lambda spring banquet in my third and final year. I was to be one of the honorees. First at cocktails, and then at the white-linen-draped table on a dais in the hotel ballroom, I went through agonies of discomfort. I was barely able to force down the overcooked peas and rubber chicken, dreading the moment when I would have to stand, be applauded, and receive a stiff parchment signifying that I'd won the Anna Augusta Von Helmholtz Phelan award for my short fiction. Thankful that I was not expected to speak, I took the parcel handed me and, had it been possible, would have pressed my left wrist and rendered myself invisible. Wonderful comic book, that. Wonderful heroine, Invisible Scarlet O'Neil.

Why this brutal self-punishment should have accompanied my every moment in the sun was to be a matter of much discussion in later years of psychoanalysis. In that spring of 1957 I could only suffer.

The difficulty pursued me to New York. It wasn't as if I got no help from the writers all around me. In the early days of his tenure, and mine, at the magazine, Paul Brodeur was in the throes of his first novel. His office was directly behind my desk, which afforded us lots of opportunity to compare notes. Paul discovered that, in true *My Sister Eileen* fashion, I had a novel, too. Its first chapters lay in that very desk, in my bottom drawer. Paul did me the honor of taking it seriously and set up a meeting for me with Seymour Lawrence, a publisher just beginning his own imprint at Delacorte. Mr. Lawrence and I had a drink together at the Harvard Club after he'd read a chapter or so. He was impressed, he said, and would look forward to seeing more.

The novel in the drawer, instead of being completed and shown to the encouraging Seymour Lawrence, was discarded in a melodramatic gesture during a trip home to Minnesota in 1963. Before going down to visit Mother and Dad, I arranged to have a drink at the Radisson in Minneapolis with my old professor Morgan Blum, to whom I had sent the novel in progress. He wasted no time in delivering his opinion. "I am very disappointed in you, Janet." His finger tapped the manuscript, which he'd hauled out of his battered briefcase. "I used to admire the honesty of your writing very much." (He had, after all, arranged for me to win the fiction prize seven years before.) "Now," he continued, "you are not only smoking with a cigarette holder, you are *writing* with one. I used to feel the humanity of the parents and adolescents you wrote about. These people!" Another tap. "I wouldn't want to spend a moment with these people, and I don't see how you can expect any reader to waste time with them." There was more, but that was the burden of the message.

I protected myself from the full force of it, making a semigraceful retreat from the hotel. I didn't know it then, but it would be the last time I was ever to see Professor Blum. He wrote me an ill-typed note from a hospital bed in Shreveport later that year. After describing at length the indignities he had suffered from a stroke, he said he hoped to be able to get home to New Orleans to die. Within a month, he got his wish.

For me, once home in Austin, there was no more delay. I spread the manuscript out on the kitchen table and reread it. The truth of what Morgan Blum had said, and the pain of acknowledging it, took me by force. I had one of those moments of renunciation I thought happened only in Henry James. It was as though each previous positive reinforcement of my talent had only been waiting for a really resounding piece of negative criticism. Before it, I lost any confidence I'd had and yielded to the negative view, giving up without a struggle. I gathered the manuscript in my arms, went out the back door, and threw it in the garbage can. After closing down that lid, I no longer dreamed of becoming a novelist. But I never lost the sense that inwardly, in some essential way, I belonged in the writing game.

A quite unexpected booster of my low morale as a would-be writer and a definite vote for my being "one of them" was my friend and longtime lunch companion Joseph Mitchell.

Among his peers at *The New Yorker,* Joseph Mitchell was the most admired writer of fact in the magazine's history. The articles he turned in from 1937 to 1964 were not numerous, but they managed to give sharp, clear pictures of whole worlds now largely passed from the scene: the old Bowery, the New York Harbor life of tugboats and shad fishermen, the Fulton Fish Market, and the old neighborhoods and graveyards of Brooklyn and Staten Island. In them he created indelible portraits of Irish barflies, lowlifes and prostitutes, Scandinavian sea captains and Italian fishmongers, and a Gypsy subculture residing in Manhattan—people he defied any reader to denigrate by identifying them as "little people": "They're as big as you are, whoever you are," he admonished.

His fact pieces, some of which were collected in *McSorley's Wonderful Saloon* in 1943, were recognized by other writers as models of their kind and have since been identified as precursors of the nonfiction novel and the new journalism, terms coined by Truman Capote and Tom Wolfe to describe what they had been doing when they wrote *In Cold Blood* and *The Kandy-Kolored Tangerine-Flake*

Streamline Baby. Of course, incorporating into nonfiction such fictional techniques as foreshortening, dialogue, and artfully arranged scenes structured so as to bring out underlying themes was a method that had been employed not only by Mitchell but by A. J. Liebling, Lillian Ross, and numerous other *New Yorker* writers (and, Joe told me, by newspapermen writing features and sports) for decades. After Capote and Wolfe discovered it in the 1960s, the method was used to good effect by Hunter Thompson and others, including Norman Mailer in *The Armies of the Night*. But no one's employment of it surpassed Mitchell's.

Joe could cover the life of a historic Irish bar by cataloging in vivid detail the hundred years' worth of yellowing photographs and framed memorabilia that lined its walls. And his drawing of character through speech and gesture in "Professor Sea Gull" was worthy of the Royal Shakespeare Company. The "Professor" was Joe Gould, a Village vagrant, fallen from high estate, who cadged drinks by asking patrons to support his epic writing project, an "Oral History of the World." Gould told Joe that this "Oral History" was "my rope and my scaffold, my bed and my board, my wife and my floozy, my wound and the salt on it, my whiskey and my aspirin, and my rock and my salvation. It is the only thing that matters a damn to me. All else is dross." Joe's marginal people may have been eccentric, but they were never cute. The Gypsy scam artist in "The King of the Gypsies" is a case in point: Joe follows her through a *hokkano baro* (wallet switch) in which she systematically fleeces an old woman of her life savings by preying on her fear of cancer. It is bone chilling.

Joseph Mitchell was a slender, handsome, straight-featured man of average height whose hair silvered early and seemed to go with his impeccable tailoring and courtly southern manners. When he died, in 1996, *The New Yorker* filled five pages with three generations of *New Yorker* contributors pouring out their tributes. That Joe, a writer of clearly superior talent, was known to be struggling with a monumental writer's block, which prevented anything of his from appearing after 1964, only seemed to increase the sympathy and esteem of his fellows.

He had a distinctive way of speaking, too, that one of his admiring chroniclers described as "stammering with a marvelous coherence"—one sentence never quite getting completed "before the next . . . tumbled from his brain."

When I was the eighteenth-floor receptionist, I saw a good deal of Joe. Not at first, since his office was on twenty and there was not much visiting between floors. However, we happened to fall into conversation on the F train one evening as he was traveling the four stops down to his home in Greenwich Village and I was going downtown by the same route to attend a graduate seminar in the Elizabethan lyric at NYU. Joe remembered that encounter and used it as part of the letter of recommendation I asked him to write for my application to the NYU doctoral program. (It would take me fifteen years to earn that PhD—but more of that later.) He said the passion I expressed for Shakespeare's courtship sonnets on that occasion had impressed him as the mark of a potential scholar, and remarked that it was all the more impressive because it followed eight hours' labor at a not very relaxing hub of journalistic industry. This must have been in about 1968. Our innocent yet not quite innocent friendship really began in earnest in 1972 when we were part of a group of people who left a gallery showing of the *New Yorker* artist Ed Koren's work to have drinks at Costello's, a bar (and former speakeasy) originally located under the tracks of the Third Avenue El.

The place had long been a hangout for *New Yorker* writers: John McNulty, James Thurber, and Joe Liebling among many others, including Dorothy Parker and Edmund Wilson. Something somebody said prompted me to paraphrase Lily the cloakroom maid in Joyce's story "The Dead." "Oh the men nowadays is only all palaver and what they can get out of ya," said I. Joe, whom I later discovered to be an enthusiastic member of the James Joyce Society, attending meetings every month or so in the upstairs rooms of the Gotham Book Mart, perked up immediately and, for the rest of the night, directed his attention exclusively and intensely to me. Although we did not have a copy of *Dubliners* before us, nothing would do but that we should go over "The Dead" nearly line by line—both of us having read it many times—in order that we might trace the way Joyce moves the story most beautifully and meaningfully toward Gabriel's epiphany, with the snow falling and casting its universal glow of reconciliation generally, "all over Ireland" (symbolizing, we agreed, the descent of the Holy Spirit).

From then until I left the magazine in 1978 we had lunch together every Friday. (The exceptions were during the term I taught up at Vassar, when, because my classes were on Friday, we switched to Monday.) When it became clear that my lunches with Joe were to be a regular thing, I thought it only polite to offer to pay my own way. Joe laughed and said it was all taken care of—he was paying for them out of his "Scandinavian royalties."

I learned a great deal from Joe in the course of those luncheons, about his enthusiasm for writers other than Joyce, among them Siegfried Sassoon and Kafka. I also heard a fair amount from him about his own work. Some of the intensity and humor of our mutual involvement in these conversations is captured in the photo Jill Krementz took of us at the fiftieth anniversary party. There we stand—much too close. So inappropriate. It is February 21, 1975, in a ballroom at the Plaza Hotel. *The New Yorker* is celebrating its own birthday, as it does every year, only instead of being basically a supper-dance after office hours, usually at the St. Regis, this year everybody is in formal attire and the waiters are passing glasses of champagne. Jill Krementz, a photographer who often supplied the author photos for book jackets, is snapping photos of the event at the Plaza in a low-key, unobtrusive way. Joe and I are clearly not even aware that our picture is being taken. We found out only months later when we were—as was everyone on the staff—offered the opportunity to buy five-by-seven black-and-white glossies, as many as we wanted, or could afford, at Ms. Krementz's price of twelve dollars apiece.

Joe is looking his usual dapper self, while I am in my "babe" mode, blond hair drawn back in a chignon, wearing a slinky gown of floor-length black jersey, the hem just touching my black suede pumps. I am holding my glass of champagne at a dangerous angle, nearly tipping the contents over the brim. Joe is much more firmly in control of his goblet, but as I happen to know, that is only because the contents of his are no more tipsiness-producing than good-quality ginger ale. We stand leaning intimately into one another no doubt partly for better audibility in the noisy ballroom, but a much funnier explanation is provided in the "caption" Joe presented to me as a farewell present when I left the magazine.

May 18, 1978

Dear Jan:

It is entirely possible that some people may not believe it, but what is going on in this picture, as you and I know, is a discussion between two Bible students. An exegetical discussion. My recollections of some of the events at The New Yorker's Fiftieth Anniversary party are quite hazy (after all, it was over three years ago), but I distinctly remember that just before Jill Krementz took this picture you and I were talking about the New Testament and you interpreted a certain verse in Galatians, I think it was, as seen in the light of a similar verse in Second Thessalonians, and at the exact moment Jill took the picture I was telling you how very much I admired your interpretation.

As ever,
Joe Mitchell

Joe thought I should frame the picture and caption and hang them in my new office when I got to the University of Cincinnati, where I was headed to an assistant professorship. Perhaps foolishly, I regarded them as too personal and hung them in my office at home instead. The real cream of Joe's jest is that it held a good degree of truth. Whatever we may have been saying in that moment at the party, a lot of our conversation over the six years or so when we met on those Fridays and lunched together, concerned, if not biblical, certainly literary passages, having to do with whatever books the two of us happened to be reading at the time. Indeed, our long quasi-platonic movable feast was made up largely of book talk.

Joe was having a problem with drinking in those days, and a few times after that evening at Costello's he called me at home or simply showed up at my door and came in for some rather lachrymose talk about Joyce and the dead and Irish literature and his many topics of interest. These were very uncomfortable visits from my point of view. I had a much-loved alcoholic father who still caused me great pain from time to time in consequence of his being unable to handle drink. To have attracted the attentions of an older man I admired (who was an unsuitable companion for me not only because he was old enough to be my father but because he was married), and to have him, too, turn out to be a drinker, seemed a pattern I was destined to repeat over and over in my life. At the University of Minnesota it was a professor of sociology; in New York thus far it had been not only Joe but half a dozen other writers and editors from the magazine. Here, there was greater confusion and pain for me than there had to be, since it was I who kept getting my father into the act.

I insisted that these nighttime visits stop, and after that, things went much better for our friendship; gradually it took the form of a daytime hour or two spent discussing poetry, drama, reportage, and fiction. We even called them our "literary lunches," and at some point in the 1970s I came in for some special treatment because of them. Harriet Walden was Miss Terry's successor as manager of the secretarial staff. It was part of her mandate to accommodate senior writers' predilections whenever possible. Mrs. Walden recognized the ritual of these Friday lunches as so important to keeping Mr. Mitchell happy that she always instructed my lunch-hour replacement to eat early so as not to miss her midday meal if I were to come back, say, half an hour or even an hour late. How do I know that this consideration was being shown not to me but to Mr. Mitchell? I don't. It was just one of a thousand little points about my job and my role at the magazine that were tacitly understood. I may have made them all up. But I don't think so.

In the early years the places we went were already long venerated as lunch spots by Joe and his pal Joe Liebling. The two of them once took me to their favorite seafood restaurant, the Red Devil, on West Forty-Eighth Street. There they thought it great fun to see me squirm as the waiter brought their order for me: baby squid prepared in its own ink, a hairy concoction that seemed to sprout seaweed and feelers and eyes. Everything at the Red Devil got served in its own ink, or its own shell, or with its spine and bones intact. There was no such thing at the Red Devil as eater-friendly food. Bibs were routine, and old-timers like the two Joes knew how to dismantle, debone, deshell, and generally suck the daylights out of all the creatures of the deep that came before them. I was mightily relieved when the Red Devil lost its lease and was forced to close.

Our next stop was the Blue Ribbon, a general favorite with *New Yorker* writers, and I had gone there with Brendan Gill and others. But after Liebling's death and the closing of their old haunt on Forty-Eighth Street, Joe and I often sought out this ancient German *Brauhaus* on West Forty-Ninth as a welcome refuge. Other ethnic restaurants followed, like the Teheran on West Forty-Fourth between Fifth and Sixth, a Middle Eastern restaurant, where the little lamb croquettes and dolma never varied and always pleased. There was also a Greek restaurant called the Parthenon on Eighth Avenue between Forty-Sixth and Forty-Seventh Streets, which hung on long after the Blue Ribbon was demolished for new construction. Here the waiters were old and tended toward the surly ("No! No more roast lamb! Too late!"). But Joe would only smile at me behind the huge grease-stained menu and drawl, "As my mama would say, 'We'll just have to rahse above it.'" The Parthenon served a lovely lemon soup, excellent lamb (when we were not too late) and new potatoes, rice in grape leaves, and baklava or, even nicer, kataifi, a honey-and-nut mixture in a shredded wheat–like base.

While on our luncheon circuit, Joe always insisted that I have a drink, conveying the idea that even if he was "on the wagon" it gave him pleasure to know that others could still enjoy a glass of chilled retsina at the Parthenon or appropriate white wines with our seafood at the Red Devil. We would often arrive separately, a gesture, I think, toward discretion, should our regular departures together through the lobby of the *New Yorker* office building be noticed and gossiped about. (As indeed we all gossiped about the frequently sighted comings and goings of Lillian Ross and Mr. Shawn, arm in arm.)

One day as Joe arrived for our lunch at the Blue Ribbon, his color was ashen. I asked him why he was so pale and sweaty and looked so unwell. He told me that he was the victim of really vicious migraines and that he felt one coming on that noontime. "I even know what *brought* it on," he said, wrinkling his nose and leaning forward in the confiding posture that often accompanied his most intensely felt revelations. The cause had been Zoë, as I shall call her here. She was the second wife of a rather famous professor who had written for *The New Yorker* from time to time. His first wife was an even more famous writer, known mainly because one of her *New Yorker* short stories was an often-anthologized favorite with students of high school and college English. Joe told me that soon after the professor was widowed he married one of his students, Zoë. Five years later, the professor, too, died. Joe went on: "For some reason—well, it was a great deal my own fault for feeling that I ought to provide a sympathetic shoulder—Zoë formed a habit—I was barely aware of it until it was too late to back out of it easily—of coming in on the train every month or two and dropping by my office to ask me if I would take her to lunch, which very soon began to be a burden to me, and when I heard from her this morning that she was coming into town—and even though I was able to avoid lunch—I wasn't altogether able to avoid a drop-in visit to my office, a visit of the most exquisite torture." Here Joe paused for a full stop before winding up. "And *that* is what brought on this goddamned migraine."

I reconstruct the breathless sentences as best I can, but I am sure they were better constructed as they came, fully edited, tumbling out of Joe's mouth. Distraught as he was, he insisted on staying and seeing me have a proper meal and would not leave until I had finished. He even had a cup of coffee himself, because he very much wanted one in any case, but also because it was thought to bring relief to sufferers of migraine by opening the blood vessels of the brain.

After the death of Joe's wife (his beloved Therese, always pronounced reverently by Joe as "Tair-EHZ"), our luncheon repertoire expanded. Joe would find that he was not expected at either his daughter Elizabeth's or his daughter Nora's of a Saturday—he was, I believe, regularly in their company on Sundays—and so would call to see if I was free. We then made pilgrimages to places like Green-Wood Cemetery in Brooklyn and to restaurants important to Joe the travel time to which couldn't be accommodated during the week, even by the relaxed standards of my office lunch hours. I remember having soft-shell crabs at Gage and Tollner, shad roe at Sloppy Louie's, lutefisk at a Norwegian restaurant in Greenpoint. The South Street Seaport was an abomination to Joe, but the waterfront had been *his* scene, and he took me for a scornful look around at what was left of it. On another occasion we paid a mournful visit to Bleeck's on Fortieth Street, even though he was on the wagon at the time, because the old newspaper hangout he'd loved from his days on *The World* and the *Herald Tribune* was about to close. He made sure that I had a Dewar's and soda and that I took my time about it.

One day we neither ate nor drank but stopped by Grace Episcopal—a lovely church on lower Broadway where Joe was a vestryman. I could never quite get a handle on Joe's degree of religious faith. It seemed to me that he found it easier to admire the *Book of Common Prayer* for its excellent prose than to suspend his disbelief over the key points in its creed. He did, however, take a considerable interest in the fact that I was not only ready to identify myself as a believer but also served on the church council at my Lutheran church in Midtown Manhattan. True, it was a congregation so advanced in its views that it would have been practically unrecognizable out in Iowa, where I was born. I also served on the jazz committee (which involved trips up to Duke Ellington's house, birthday parties for Eubie Blake, and chicken and waffles on 125th Street), participated in a young people's play-reading group heavily weighted toward theater of the absurd, and attended discussions more theologically sympathetic to Martin Buber's *I and Thou* than to the catechism of Martin Luther—though we did like to quote the instruction Luther gave to his children to "sin boldly" because the Lord loves a sinner. I think Joe considered me something of an oddity, combining in one (he thought) shapely body a fondness for both bohemia and Buber. Well, how about him? As he liked to say whenever a pot-kettle situation arose, "The one called the other one one and come to find out he was one hisself!"

Other restaurants—in which we had migraine-free lunches—included the Cortile, running between Forty-Third and Forty-Fourth Streets in the building next door to the *New Yorker* offices. Chosen mainly for comic relief, or to avoid inclement weather, the Cortile was a most unconvincing attempt to re-create a Creole establishment. At the opposite end of the aesthetic spectrum, there was a wonderful backroom Italian restaurant called something like Casa Roma on West Forty-Fifth Street toward Sixth. This place was so seductive, its menu so glorious, its waiting staff so European in its quiet deference and efficiency, and its atmosphere so conducive to long talks and gustatory pleasures that my lunch hour when we ate there invariably stretched to two hours instead of one. After that place, too, closed, much to our sorrow, we began to substitute an old French restaurant, Pierre au Tunnel, which Joe liked because it served tripe and brains, the mammalian equivalent of the repellent, squishy dishes of vaunted Red Devil memory, or an equally old Italian restaurant, La Strada, in the West Forties farther over toward Eighth in the theater district. I would drink Lillet at the French restaurant and Punt e Mes or Martini & Rossi at the Italian place before the glass of red or white wine Joe encouraged me to have with our entrée, so those Friday meals were full European midday breaks. Though the food at virtually all the places Joe chose (the utilitarian Cortile excepted) was excellent and we took it and the pleasure it gave us very seriously, the real feast of these occasions, for me certainly and, I like to think, for Joe, too, was the accompanying talk.

What did we talk about?

Mostly we talked about death. Books, of course, but they, too, were mostly about death in one way or another. It was extraordinary, really, how many of our meetings took on the aspect of a wake. We were both solemnly and merrily celebrating and commemorating death in so many of them. On the surface it might be the death or the doom and impending death of the pub we were in or the restaurant we were in or the part of the city we were visiting. At bottom it was the death of our fathers that drew us together. Joe touched me forever by tracking down my parents' phone number in Minnesota and calling me on the day of my father's funeral. In Joe's case, he thought of his father's actual death as a second death, their falling-out over Joe's leaving the family tobacco and cotton farm to come to New York having been the first. Arrived in the city, young and grieving for his absent father, Joe had formed a close attachment to a crusty Italian fisherman, Tony Fabriziano, as I shall call him, patriarch of the Fulton Fish Market. In the late 1970s that bond, too, was threatened. Though it clung on for a few more years, the Fulton Market had already received its death sentence, and by then his old friend Tony had died under the strain. In that double death, Joe found his subject. He realized it was of this, he told me, that he had been trying to write for years—weaving into a seamless whole the passing of the old South, symbolized in the death of his father, and the passing of the old port-and-market New York, symbolized in the passing of Tony Fabriziano. A grand subject, a subject with scope and ramifications that he was willing to follow through all its twists and turns until he could not only capture it, render its sights and sounds and smells and voices, but redeem its sins, reconcile its contradictions, and elevate it like a host to heaven in praise of the Lord. Oh, Joe, what a cross you constructed for yourself, and how you crucified yourself upon it! The first ten years were the relatively easy part—it had taken Joyce seven years, and more, to write *Ulysses.* But as the first decade moved toward a second and as the notes in the drawers of his desk remained notes and refused to shape themselves into manuscript, watching it happen and listening to the note of suppressed panic in Joe's voice as he tried—and he could only occasionally bring himself to try—to talk about it, I began to catch a glimmer of what it was about his choice of subject that was defeating him. I didn't know I'd caught it, and I wouldn't know until my own struggles toward articulation would bring me face-to-face with it that it was his congenital shyness and reticence about himself and his own depths of feeling that were getting in his way.

On the one hand there was the difficulty of his trying to write two books into one. He wanted to do justice to subjects as stubbornly unmixable as oil and water; the cotton and tobacco fields of North Carolina would never smell right in the fish and saltwater and concrete and brick of Lower East Side New York. It was as if Joyce had tried to write a day in Dublin *and* a day in Trieste. Even Joyce did not try that. And those who have succeeded in moving back and forth between two disparate settings, in time and space, have done so in the frame of an epic novel held together by one consciousness. By tackling the work in journalistic terms, leaving himself out, he was depriving himself of a literary character in whom he would invest authority, the authorial point of view, a literary persona to be the teller of his tale. It was as though Joe were trying to write *War and Peace* without Pierre, *The Great Gatsby* without Nick Carraway, *Great Expectations* without Pip, *You Can't Go Home Again* without Eugene Gant. Most nearly a parallel of all, he was attempting *Remembrance of Things Past* without the youthful Marcel to register it. And however skillfully Joseph Mitchell was attempting to do it, it was defeating him, and he knew it and he couldn't do anything about it. That was painful to witness. And it is more painful still to bear witness to. Yet the story is not without its poignancy or its heroism, and there was, in the late-in-life revival of his work and his reputation with the publication of *Up in the Old Hotel,* a Pyrrhic victory of the sort that Joe's "graveyard cast of mind" and his predilection for black comedy must have relished.

Sadly for me, by that time I had morphed into Joe's next Zoë. He was exquisitely polite, but my encounters with him, rare in the years after I left New York, dwindled at last into an awkward drop-in or two. Our final meeting was an accidental encounter in the post office on Forty-Third. How painful to see in his eyes, and to hear in his stammering, apologetic tones as he spoke to me, the death of the beau ideal I had been and the onslaught of the bête noire I had become. Yet another death, and this one I would be commemorating alone.

But before we entered that long winter of our discontent with each other, there was many a springtime day. One afternoon as we left La Strada after our Friday lunch, Joe became fixated on a vine running up one of the poles holding up the canopy over the restaurant's entryway. "Wh-why, I do believe th-this is a fig tree!" He often stammered when he was excited about what he wanted to say.

We stood for some time as he fingered it, looked closely at it, from near and from a little farther away, stepping perhaps three feet back in order to see it from top to bottom. "The Italians, you know, believe the fig to have aphrodisiac powers." He glanced meaningfully at me without a trace of prurience in his glance. He was disinterestedly interested in the aphrodisiac powers of the fig. Or their reputedly aphrodisiac powers. He plucked a leaf from the cleanest, most hidden, lushest part of the twining plant, sniffed it, and rolled it in his fingers as appreciatively as a Wall Street financier might have sniffed and rolled a leaf from what was to become a hand-rolled Cuban cigar. Joe offered it to me, saying "S-niff that! Isn't that—mamm-arvvelous? F-ffeel it! A rough texture, almost like fffine ssandpaper!" I sniffed and rolled and felt and marveled. "You know, ssome people believe ZZ-Zacchaeus was s-ssitting in a ff-fig t-tree as he spoke to the C-Christ." Now we were in an area Joe truly loved. He liked nothing better than to combine the sacred and the profane, the mind and the body, the way Yeats had noted the seat of love being so near the seat of excrement in the human structure—a sure sign of intention for their interweaving on the part of the Creator.

As we progressed on our slow perambulation back to the office, I stuffed the fig leaf into the pocket of my raincoat. It was a coat I very much admired, a terra-cotta trench coat in which I looked particularly well, I imagined, with the collar up around my face and my hands stuffed in its deep pockets. I formed the habit of taking out the fig leaf and replacing it in the pocket after I had had the coat cleaned. I kept that coat for years, and when at last I brought it out of the closet to send it to the thrift shop, I stuck my hand into the pocket to remove any personal items, and the dried fig leaf—long since bereft of its odor but redolent with memories of Joe—came out and nestled in my hand.

The religious nature of our meals together sometimes approached moments of Joycean epiphany. On one occasion I recall especially, Joe and I were seated in the curve of the red banquette in the rear of the street-floor dining room of the Teheran. As our food arrived, I was intensely involved with the talk Joe and I were having; at the same time I was keenly aware of the flavors of the dolma and the lamb croquettes that were the restaurant's signature dish. The spices of the lamb and the silky texture of the grape leaves and the bite of the dry white wine and the excitement of our finding exactly the right words of praise for the story we were considering (I think it was Joyce again, that gritty symbol of reality in *Dubliners,* "Clay") combined into a wondrous fifth substance that seemed to take place in another dimension.

Those were "highs" for me, but I mustn't neglect my equally keen awareness that Joe's customary psychic place was more likely to be de profundis, or, as he called it, his "graveyard cast of mind." It was no accident that his writing in the years just before the writer's block shut him down altogether dwelt on the bottom of the harbor and the rats who lived there as in a watery grave. I found deeply emblematic of his depression over the block Joe's admiration for a story of Kafka's called "The Burrow"—a story of relentless gloom involving a rodent enmeshed in a series of underground tunnels from which he neither could nor wished to escape. Only my esteem for Joe sustained me to see "The Burrow" through to the end of one complete reading. It has been beyond my power ever to look into it again.

It was at another lunch at the Teheran that Joe gave me some cherished praise for a story I had written while a freshman at the University of Minnesota. It was a thinly disguised fictionalization of something that had happened to me when I was eleven and living with my family in a trailer on the West Pacific Coast Highway in Long Beach, California. I spent a good deal of time alone in those days while my mother and father cut expenses at the restaurant they were running by waiting on tables and covering the cashier desk themselves. In the way lonely children have of latching onto surrogate families, I had begun to spend time with a boy about my own age in his family's apartment on the first floor of the modest apartment house in front of our trailer's mooring place. Jerry and I played game after game of Monopoly, and I called my story "Monopoly." The climax of the action came with our discovery on the kitchen floor one evening of the convulsed body of Jerry's mother, a suicide. My idealization of Jerry's as the perfect family, the family I did not have, was shattered. But the story, of course, projects the devastation onto Jerry. The passage that Joe praised, and to which he alluded often in our later lunches, evidently possessed merits of which I had no inkling. It described the desolation of the vacant lot next to the rear of the apartment building, where police discovered an empty container of rat poison—a particularly gruesome and caustic way for the dead woman to have induced her own end. The passage figures in the story as a metaphor for Jerry's mother's real life. But it was the vacant lot that so enchanted Joe. He never let me forget that lot and how much he admired my depiction of it.

The day came—we were again in the Teheran—when a literary figure arose in our discussion about whom we disagreed. The year was 1974, the figure was E. L. Doctorow, and the work was *Ragtime.* It had just come out, and I praised it as wildly and playfully original, a work of genius. Joe saw it as totally false from start to finish, the work of a charlatan. Inwardly I quailed at finding myself in dispute with a man whom I considered my mentor. I was appalled at the precarious limb on which I suddenly found myself perched; in my nervousness I started to babble about the five parts of Cicero's rhetoric by which to measure the merits of a work—*dispositio, elocutio, memoria, pronunciato,* and *inventio*—even going so far, though I had never had a lesson in Latin in my life, as presuming to give the terms in Latin. Not content with this display of rank pomposity, I said that furthermore, it was this last trait, invention (something told me to pronounce it "in-WHEN-tio") that nobody else seemed to be doing any longer and that had so impressed me about *Ragtime.* I told myself I was doing this for Doctorow, but I was just too damned scared to say it was me saying it for me. It may have been the first tiny rift that would eventually demote me from my position as hallowed Lady of the Literary Lunch to a second Zoë.

As the years went on and I became more the horn-rimmed academic than the Scandinavian princess (or the blond babe) of his dreams, my meetings with Joe became ever fewer until they were reduced to the occasional espresso. When Sheila McGrath entered his life, they ceased altogether. Sheila was the office manager, a striking woman with thick auburn hair, which she wore in a single braid. I had been very close to her at the time of my father's death—she had just lost her father, too, a well-known figure in Sheila's home in Saint John's, Newfoundland. We had several nights of scotch and

Tony Bennett (the album he made with Bill Evans) and told each other the story of our dads. Sheila's gift for dry humor must have been a good fit for Joe's graveyard cast of mind. So I thought there was something poetic and right about it, as if he had moved from "The Dead" of *Dubliners* to find a companion for his own version of *Finnegans Wake.*

Remembering Muriel

I met Muriel Spark for the first time in 1961, when she was assigned an office on "my floor." At the time she was seeing *The Prime of Miss Jean Brodie* into press. Although four or five earlier works of fiction had brought her some recognition in Britain, it was her novel of the sinister Scottish schoolteacher that was to earn her international fame. It also broke a precedent at the magazine as the first time a piece of fiction was to make up so much of the editorial content of an issue. In 1964, Mrs. Spark (as I called her then) asked me to "moonlight" as her private secretary. She told me she was being inundated with mail from fans and from the young men she termed her "priestlings": the numerous Catholic theology students who wrote to her—she was a famous convert—wanting her to attend their ordinations. I was to handle her personal correspondence, keeping the priestlings, and the world in general, at bay in order to let her get on with her work. As she wrote in her autobiography, "'Fame's dizzy heights' are more often than not a great pain in the neck."

I saw her for the last time in Arezzo, when we had lunch in the stately old dining room of the Hotel Minerva in June 2004. By then we had become something more than employer and employee but something less than intimate friends. My dealings with her, even when I worked for her, had more to do with something we liked about each other than with her as a famous writer. For years she sent me copies of her books and I sent her my far fewer academic publications. We wrote every Christmas, and we were always glad to see each other. In the shadow of her death in April 2006, I am conscious, as I never was while she lived, that our connection was a remarkable if slender thing.

Muriel Spark was a tiny woman, and in the early days of our acquaintance, she possessed a headful of red-blond ringlets, a fluting voice, and the features of a porcelain shepherdess. To the English ear her voice always retained a Scots accent, but to me it seemed that of a well-educated English person. There was, in any case, a good deal of music in it. She loved nice clothes, and even when she was working hard on the nitty-gritty editorial chores of getting galleys prepared for the printer, she would wear clingy print dresses of Liberty silk and lovely, shapely Italian shoes with small heels. She appreciated good jewelry and had sizable bills with David Webb to prove it. I expect that she learned a good deal about the subject when she spent several years in the 1940s working at *Argentor*, the publication of the National Jewellers' Association in Britain. Her petite figure was the result of a dramatic change that she brought to bear upon her own life in her late twenties. She had been, in a description the *New Yorker* contributor and collector of literary scuttlebutt Brendan Gill delighted in telling around the office, "positively obese" and the very picture of a drab bookworm when she came to postwar London to seek her way (having shed a husband in South Africa). Then, in Brendan's telling, she began to work for a famous poet. ("Was it T. S. Eliot? Was it one of the Sitwells?" Actually, it was the *Poetry Review,* a venue for the work of not one poet but many.) "And before you knew it," Brendan would recount enthusiastically, "she had taken over the poet, taken over his office, brought her weight down by three stone, turned herself from an ugly duckling into a swan, and published a literary masterpiece to boot!" The masterpiece was her novel *Memento Mori.*

Muriel did not move into the eighteenth floor in a formal way until 1964, the year I began working for her. Her earlier stint had found her using only a borrowed cubicle. She was assigned one of the most desirable locations on eighteen, a corner office formerly belonging to A. J. Liebling, who had died on December 28, 1963. She immediately organized a paint job (a French blue was soon in place on the walls), and she added an oriental rug, a sofa cover, throw pillows, an armchair, and a well-framed oil over the couch. This unaccustomed attention to personal comfort and even luxury of surroundings set off a minor revolution. Requests flowed into the office manager from irate writers who demanded something other than the regulation gray walls with dirty Venetian blinds at the windows and straight wooden chairs and linoleum floors and metal filing cabinets that had constituted the norm for as long as the eighteenth floor had been in existence. They were given the OK to do it "as Mrs. Spark did it"—that is, to do it themselves. This area was the *New Yorker* domain for writers and a very few cartoonists, with me, the facilitator, in a sort of wide spot in the hall by the back stairs. A year or so earlier, some attempt had been made to create a "conversation pit" beneath the stairwell connecting us to the editorial floor above. It was not a success. Liebling, eyeing the dusty, rust-colored love seat and two matching chairs, said it reminded him of a third-class lounge on a second-class ship.

Mrs. Spark was careful not to request my services until after office hours or during lunchtime. Over the next year and a half I disappointed many seekers of favors, refusing many invitations of one kind or another in her name and in the cause of preserving her time for her writing. One correspondence she dealt with herself consisted of the light blue aerograms from her son Robin. "Set that aside," she'd say when she saw one of those. "He's asking for money again." This struck me as cold, but then I was just at that moment learning of Robin's existence. I had had no idea she had a son. Years later her autobiography would tell the story of how difficult it was for Muriel to get passage out of Africa in 1944, during the still lethal days of World War II. She records having left Robin in the care of Dominican nuns. She would also write of how she later brought him to Edinburgh and left him there with her parents, seeing him only intermittently then and after she was able to swing a place for him in a good English boarding school. Perhaps because he reminded her of the disastrous marriage that took her to Africa in the first place, Robin never evoked a maternal response in Muriel, yet she always found a way to see to his care. The astonishing transformation she had brought about in her own circumstances must have been equally difficult to pull off. Small wonder it was not accomplished without a breakdown.

Sometime in the early 1950s, as I understand it, when she was hounded out of her editorial job at the *Poetry Review,* she had a nervous collapse and lived for a time in a cloistered situation run by the Catholic Church. It was out of that experience that a new Muriel

Spark emerged, a Catholic convert who would remain in the church for the rest of her life. She also became, during that incarceration, an artist who wrote the first of her many novels, *The Comforters,* about a young woman who has a mental breakdown that grants her mystical visions.

Opening her mail, as well as answering it, gained me insight into Muriel's tastes and how she spent her time. In spite of all the refused invitations, she saw a great many people in a social way, often escorted by one of three or four personable young men she came across in her publisher's office or in that of her agent Ivan von Auw. She saw Brendan Gill, the *New Yorker* poetry editor Howard Moss, and Ved Mehta, the Indian author and autobiographer, who was then writing on the Oxford philosophers. She saw other writers like Anne Fremantle and Shirley Hazzard and Shirley Hazzard's husband, Francis Steegmuller, a Flaubert translator. Her apartment in the Beaux Arts Hotel—a spacious one-bedroom done up in shades of ivory and baby blue with Louis Quinze furniture—placed her in the immediate environs of the Secretariat Building, though I don't believe she socialized much with the visiting dignitaries. The UN setting took a sly hit in the title of her 1973 novel, *The Hothouse by the East River,* which was, however, only marginally set in New York and was, among other things, a fictionalization of her postwar intelligence work for MI6.

All these high-profile social contacts notwithstanding, it was my impression that Muriel was quite lonely and isolated in her New York years; she sometimes asked me, when I was dropping off typing or picking up new assignments, to stay for a cocktail before I went home. And when, by some fluke, she found herself unoccupied for Thanksgiving in 1965, she wound up having that holiday with my brother and me and some other friends of mine at Keens Chop House. She insisted on picking up the tab and took everybody home in her chauffeured limousine. That I remember no single witty thing she said on that occasion—or indeed much of anything else about it—I suspect has more to do with the excellent dry martinis at Keens than with the absence of any memorable talk. When Muriel was around, the talk was always memorable. She was, for example, very funny about the priestlings and the "sweet certainty" they evinced that her convert's zeal would inspire in her the desire to drop the novel she was composing and travel to the far reaches of West Virginia to see them being ordained.

Summer was my vacation time (eight weeks, four of them with pay), and someone from the typing pool was tapped to fill in for me with Muriel. In 1966, when I mentioned that my summer plans included six weeks of study at Oxford, she was enthusiastic. She told me that she would have liked to go to university herself, if she'd had the chance, but that the family coffers in Edinburgh would stretch only so far as a business course, which had led her to a clerkship in a local department store.

One day in early June, I showed her a notice she'd received in the mail for something called the Sussex Lifeboat Ball. I remarked on the posh nature of this event and asked her if she had a special fondness for lifeboats. She laughed and corrected me; it was not the boats she was fond of but a racehorse named Lifeboat, of which she was a one-eighth owner. She cocked her head and looked at me: "Aren't you going to be at Oxford during July? That is not so very far from Petworth House." A glint in her eye, she asked, "Would you like to go?" I said I'd be enchanted, whereupon she dictated the following letter:

> Captain the Hon. V. M. Wyndham-Quin, R.N.
> Lifeboat House
> 42 Grosvenor Gardens
> London, S.W. 1
> England
>
> Dear Captain Wyndham-Quin,
>
> Thank you so much for your letter and notices of the Sussex Lifeboat Ball, which I so much regret having to miss. I shall be working in New York all summer . . .
>
> However, a young American friend of mine, Miss Janet Groth, is studying at Oxford and would, I know, love to attend the ball. She's a charming girl and I know she'll enjoy it. If you will send me a ticket for two, I will see that she gets it in good time. I shall let you know if I find any other friends who would like to have tickets. Meantime, I enclose a check which includes a small donation to the Lifeboat Institution.
>
> With best wishes,
>
> Yours sincerely,
> Muriel Spark

A couple of weeks later I brought her Captain Wyndham-Quin's handwritten reply, noting his thanks for her donation to the Lifeboat Institution and his concluding paragraph, which announced that he would "look forward to seeing Janet Groth and one of her friends" at the ball. With the cheek that only the clueless possess, I told her I needed two more tickets so that not only an escort with a motor car but my good friends from London, Peter and Winifred Wroe, could attend.

The Wroes were part of a transplanted merry band of Yorkshiremen I met on the boat train from Paris to Calais on my first trip to Europe in 1959. We had bonded while making up rude lyrics to "Blue Moon" and staving off seasickness in the saloon of the Channel steamer. By the time we pulled into Victoria near midnight, we were fast friends. They took me home to stay on their couch, and I had been staying on their couch on every return visit to London since. I couldn't imagine going to a county ball without them. When I posed this condition to Muriel, she smiled and said, "I think that might be arranged." We shot off another letter to Captain Wyndham-Quin and received his response in the next mail. Tickets for Miss Groth and three of her friends were enclosed.

I went to Ohrbach's, a now defunct discount store on Thirty-Fourth Street, and found the ball gown of my dreams; it had a white top and a teal-and-white floral skirt with a pink bow at the waist. I drew a picture of it for Muriel.

My charter flight to England, enrollment at Oxford University, and settling into borrowed lodgings in a Mr. Throckmorton's rooms in Exeter College all went off without a hitch. The day before I was to leave for London, I received an amusing letter from Winifred Wroe about her trials in coming up with a pumpkin and a Prince Charming. In the end she'd borrowed John Lansdale, with permission from his best girl, Agnes. John would, she wrote, "speed back from Cornwall to escort and transport." In addition to his possessing an Austin automobile and a tuxedo, Winifred claimed he was "excellent at whispering behind potted palms." And although she admitted to one hitch—"he cannot dance"—she assured me that he would be "delighted to hold you whilst you dance."

I later shared this flavor-of-the-occasion letter with Muriel, showed her the accompanying photos, and reported on our drive at high speed from Camden Town to Petworth House. I told her, too, of our late arrival—we just missed being presented to Princess Marina, which was all to the good, since my curtsy was thought by Winifred to "need work." I spoke of Winifred's and my inspection of the ladies' powder room, where a discreet placard told us that this chamber and bath were occupied by the violinist Yehudi Menuhin when he came to stay for the weekend. Then it was on to Buck's fizzes in the great hall and a tour of the house, admiring the Adam fireplaces as we went. John, while not *my* Prince Charming, was indeed charming, and with his high brow and wispy blond beard, he reminded me of a prince—Prince Myshkin in Dostoyevky's novel. After our tour of the premises, we paid a brief visit to the nightclub, where John held me in a rather dance-like position as I took a few twirls under the neon lighting specially installed for the occasion. At around 1:00 a.m. all the guests were invited to the gallery—a sort of indoor terrace with white furniture and, yes, potted palms—for a champagne supper of caviar and cucumber sandwiches. By two thirty we joined the last of the string of cars drawn up to the porte cochere and rolled down a graveled drive to wend our way back to London on the county roads of Sussex. Muriel said that by all indications and as county balls went, I'd had a good one.

While a far cry from an English county ball, I was able to return the invitation to the dance the following year. My coconspirator in the matter was Andrena (Andy) Bear, a leggy, sensational-looking blond who worked as the editor's secretary in the Talk of the Town department, whose offices, like those of On and Off the Avenue, the fashion department, were located on the eighteenth floor. Andy was a great favorite of Charles Addams and Peter De Vries and a number of the forty or so other men whose offices were on that floor. (There were half a dozen women—besides Muriel—sprinkled around, too.) These men had a good eye for beauty, and they eyed Andy with evident pleasure. On good days and in the right light I had my admirers also, and we used to kid that, had we chosen to do so, we could have created quite a scandal.

A couple of things prompted our joining forces in the creation of a summer dance. First was the impromptu *New Yorker* jazz band I had helped bring about. All I'd had to do was put the right parties together. Two cartoonists, Lee Lorenz and Warren Miller, played trumpet and cornet (and Warren occasionally sang a vocal or two in tribute to his idol Fats Waller); Paul Brodeur played clarinet; Whitney Balliett, the magazine's jazz critic, played drums; when she hosted the jam session in the solarium of her East Side town house, Daphne Hellman played the harp; and the Talk reporter Wally White sat in on piano, occasionally spelled by a *New York Times* reporter named Phil Benjamin. We always hoped *The New Yorker*'s editor in chief, William Shawn, an excellent piano player himself, would come, but he never did.

So we had the band; all we needed now was the hall. As if on cue, one of the band members, Lee Lorenz, received notice that he'd soon have to vacate his loft on Spring Street. The perfect time to hold a party there, we all agreed. Andy and I were to be the hostesses, and we had great fun with the planning. We decided to invite everyone we knew at the magazine to our "bash." Of necessity (our budgets not stretching to more elaborate arrangements), we conceived it as a strictly blue-collar affair at which we would serve hot dogs, pretzels, and mustard, with a keg and setups for the BYOB crowd. It was fixed for a summer night in June 1967, and the stage was set for a first-class Greenwich Village "scene" involving high and low alike. Sort of like the annual anniversary dance at the St. Regis, but without the business department.

Most of the editorial department and many of the cartoonists were in attendance, and the odd matchups that resulted were a source of awe and sometimes wonder. Charles Addams, whose dinner companions ran to the likes of Joan Fontaine, Drue Heinz, and Jacqueline Kennedy, turned up in a black tie and, perhaps in homage to Andy, alone. Muriel arrived with a very young and handsome blond—a gent from her agent's office, I was given to understand. She looked beautiful in a strapless yellow chiffon dress accessorized with silver stiletto slippers and a rhinestone brooch centered on its bosom. She sported some David Webb bracelets on her slender arms, and her hair was freshly done in a reddish-blond bouffant. She made a typically generous contribution to the festivities, her escort leaving at least a jeroboam of Dom Pérignon at the paper-draped bar. The band, getting the picture, launched into "Puttin' On the Ritz," and things took a decided upward turn.

The next big party I shared with Muriel was equally star studded, but in an international rather than an American vein. Muriel had moved to Italy in 1969 and engaged a series of English-speaking secretaries there until she found a permanent helpmeet, Penelope Jardine, in 1978. She continued to ask me for my assistance in dealing with her New York affairs and always sent checks to cover expenses and my services. In 1970, on a summer holiday, I was passing through Rome and received a note from Muriel inviting me to come to her "little supper."

It was definitely more elegant than any little supper I could remember, taking place, as it did, in her apartment in the Palazzo Taverna, an Italian Renaissance structure that had once been the residence of Cardinal Orsini. An opera fan and a Puccini buff, I was amazed to see through a sliver of window the battlements of the Castel Sant'Angelo, from which at the end of act 3 Floria Tosca flings herself into the Tiber. The place was longer on walk-in stone fireplaces and octagonal coffered ceilings than on windows. It seemed that cardinals in their residences preferred privacy to public views.

The guests included old *New Yorker* pals Brendan Gill and Niccolò Tucci, which was lucky because they made me feel right at home in a crowd that might otherwise have been intimidating. There were a number of deposed European royals and a sprinkling of the Cinecittà crowd. Michelangelo Antonioni talked to me as he drank a glass of white wine. He spoke about his distaste for social gatherings of this kind, having made an exception that evening because of his esteem for "cara Muriel"—a conversation translated for us by his obliging personal assistant, an American college girl from Sarah Lawrence.

The only unsettling thing about this evening was Muriel's gown, which was perhaps not quite suited to her age and station. The skirt had three fluted orange tiers, the uppermost poking out stiffly around her middle as she greeted her guests from the top of a sweeping stone staircase. Brendan Gill kissed her hand, grinned, and said, "You look like an ice cream cone," only saving her smile by adding, "good enough to eat." True, the salesperson should burn in hell for selling her that orange organza, but Muriel looked so pleased to be wearing it that all the would-be cats present at the gathering lost the will to triumph over her.

When Muriel made the arrangements to send me to the ball in Sussex, I felt like Cinderella. But as I think back on her delight in nice dresses and her frankness about the hardship she had undergone, it occurs to me that perhaps it was not I but she who was Cinderella. It just takes longer to get to the ball when you have to be your own fairy godmother. (For a period of six years during and just after the war, she had been too poor to buy any clothes at all.) To the extent that Muriel had a fairy godmother, he came in the form of Graham Greene. An admirer of her writing, Greene sent her twenty pounds a month in the period after her job at the *Poetry Review* fell through, but that was only to make ends meet.

Apart from *The Prime of Miss Jean Brodie* and other writing she sold to *The New Yorker,* I didn't read Muriel's work until I ceased being her secretary. It seems to me now that I avoided doing so out of a superstitious fear that I would learn something from it that would interfere with my perception of her as a benevolent employer. I was always coming across reviews that referred to her work as "biting," "darkly witty," and, some thought, "lacking in charity." But to me she was generous and sweet. Later I could see what they meant—in *Robinson, Memento Mori,* and most of her numerous other novels, poems, and short stories. It was not until I was asked by *Commonweal* to review her 1983 novel, *Loitering with Intent,* that I began to get a handle on what Muriel Spark the writer was all about.

In the review, I draw the analogy Muriel frequently drew herself, between artistry and criminality, noting that both the artist and the criminal like to take us by surprise. The novel is Muriel's nearest approach to a vade mecum for the study of her works. Her main character, a budding novelist named Fleur, evolves an artistic credo that fits neatly with her own. Fleur has a job editing the papers of some old society snobs and is accused of plundering these private papers (read private lives) for use in her own work. Fleur is not ready to call herself innocent of this charge: "I was aware of a *daemon* inside me that rejoiced in seeing people as they were, and not only that, but more than ever as they were, and more, and more."

Beneath its entertainments of plot and character, there is, as always in Muriel Spark novels, a spiritual discussion going on. Here, it is neatly entwined with the widely differing attitudes toward life of two famous autobiographers, Cardinal Newman and Benvenuto Cellini. Both are believers: one is a man of the cloth and an apologist for religion, the other an artist and craftsman. Fleur finds Newman's reduction of the drama of faith to "two and two only supreme and luminously self-evident beings"—himself and his Creator—in *Apologia pro vita sua* quite "neurotic." To Fleur a defrocked priest is also "a self-evident and luminous being." And, she goes on, "So are you, so is my lousy landlord and the same goes for everyone I know. You can't live with an I-and-thou relationship to God and doubt the reality of the rest of life."

Cellini, the robust Renaissance craftsman, on the other hand, has inspired Fleur's own writing, and it is particularly his trust in the material world that so delights her.

This is not to say the novel gives all the points to Cellini. Spark ultimately grants Newman the power to lead her heroine to the

Catholic faith and to the disposition of her immortal soul. But it is in Cellini's all-consuming focus on the making of art that Fleur/ Muriel announces her own aesthetic. No overt proselytizing will intrude, and all other claims will fall before it. (In this light it becomes possible to understand Muriel's imperviousness to her son's hopes that she might evince a maternal pride in his own art, his painting: "I don't think he's any good and nothing will make me say so," she informed an interviewer.) Freud fares scarcely better: "I don't hold with psychology," she once told me. Her no-nonsense approach to what in others might have been the murky stuff of psychological novels is especially apparent in *The Driver's Seat,* a novella in which the heroine seeks out her own murderer in Rome. Upon reading it I joined the army of those who regard her works as so many small, perfect, polished gems.

The best chance I had to observe Muriel outside the office or a formal gathering came about in 1989 when, in consequence of a sabbatical I spent in Italy, I was her guest for the Christmas holiday. On that occasion there did gleam forth a sighting or two of the lady's darker side. I was house-sitting in Cortona, some distance from where Muriel was staying with Penelope Jardine, her companion for the previous ten years. Nonetheless, Muriel invited me for Christmas dinner, and I made the following journal entry, on December 26, 1989, the day after I returned:

> I arrived at the station in Arezzo at 5:45 p.m. Penelope was to pick me up at six.
>
> Waiting outside the station, I shivered a bit; I was wearing only a light raincoat and the station thermometer showed six degrees Celsius. But Penelope was prompt, driving up to the curb at 6:03 in a

dusty, almost new Alfa Romeo, which I later discovered belongs to Muriel but which she doesn't drive.

Penelope, a woman of about fifty-five with a mild, pleasant face, no makeup, and short, light brown hair, shrugged off the half-hour drive involved in fetching me and the still longer drive involved in taking me back to Cortona at the end of the evening. "I expect we'll be fairly merry by then," she said. "We'll scarcely notice."

I asked how Penelope, a Scot, a sculptor and painter, had come to purchase the thirteenth-century church she and Muriel were renovating. She said that years before, when she was living in Rome, she had been told that the Catholic Church was selling many of its smaller holdings in Italy; a friend took her to the local bishop, who helped her to accomplish the purchase.

We now arrived at the walled town of Oliveto, above which the house is situated. She paused to show me a small chapel at a crossroads.

"That chapel consecrates the spot where the last plague victim died—about the period of *I promessi sposi*," she said, turning up the steep hill of their drive. "So Muriel and I like to say we live above the plague line."

Muriel, looking nice in a black chiffon skirt with a touch of what may have been feathers or fur at the hem and a beaded black mohair sweater, greeted me with a hug. Both she and Penelope seemed pleased over my present to them of Moët & Chandon. We discussed whether to have champagne immediately or wait for the other guests, deciding to wait a bit (it was just quarter of seven). Muriel said that they had been glued to the television following the swiftly unfolding events in Romania and that if I didn't mind they would like to watch the news at seven o'clock. I said I'd like to and asked what the latest information was. Both mentioned in shocked tones the mounting death toll being attributed to troops still faithful to the repressive Ceausescu, who'd been executed that afternoon. Muriel at one point broke out bitterly, "Seventy thousand dead and there the survivors sit, without so much as an aspirin."

We then ascended to Muriel's bedroom and watched a half hour of almost unrelieved bad news. Violence in the Romanian city of Timisoara. Muriel was worried about a young friend who lives there—a translator of her books—who had just had a baby. Violence in Jerusalem. Candlelit masses in the streets of Prague and Bucharest. In a brief nod to the good news of the fall of the Berlin Wall, there was a snippet of Leonard Bernstein conducting a performance of Beethoven's Ninth at the Brandenburg Gate. Then, back to the grim, with a captured kidnapper telecasting an appeal to his Italian cohorts to give themselves up and restore their victim to his family unharmed.

Afterward we came down to Penelope's bedroom/sitting room and attempted to get into a more festive frame of mind. The room was cheerful, featuring chintz and pillows and Christmas decorations. I commented on two oil portraits, asking if they were done by Penelope. I was told the one of Muriel, in profile, was. "It belongs to Penny," said Muriel. Then she added, "She hasn't given it to me." She said that the other, showing a young and dashing Penelope, had been done by a friend in Rome.

Somehow, Muriel got going on Africa—not Rhodesia, site of her unhappy marriage, but South Africa and South Africans. She became so heated about it that Penelope asked, with a laugh, "What other nationalities are there, I wonder, we can banish wholesale?" It seemed that Australians, too, aroused Muriel's ire. "I never met one who wasn't vulgar in the extreme—look at Germaine [Greer], for example, although I quite like her. I have to send word ahead if I'm going to see her to ask them to get her to please leave out the four-letter words if I'm to stay in the room with her." She looked at us fiercely: "And she *just* manages to do it." The Italians were all right, she said, because Italians "always allow for a court of appeal."

We had drinks, Irish whiskey and water for me, red wine for Muriel, and gin and tonic for Penelope. Muriel gave me a little present wrapped in stiff, brownish-maroon paper. Inside was a pottery dish, heart shaped, with a blue-and-white figure of a bird on a heart-shaped branch. "It was just a little something I saw in an antiques shop in Arezzo that I thought you might like," said Muriel.

"I love it," I said. And I did.

There were to be just two other guests, I was told. An English architect and collector of art named Frederick Fuchs (Freddie) and his friend, a young Italian named Dario, arrived bearing huge pots of pink geraniums. After a tour of the house, we gathered around a table set up in Penelope's bedroom and feasted on a four-course dinner: guinea fowl served with good local Chianti, followed by Christmas pudding and champagne.

Art was, naturally, a recurrent topic. Freddie was soon telling us how the Japanese—"the big buyers nowadays"—were making it possible for collectors like him to own works by Italian masters; it seemed the masters were experiencing a depressed market because the Japanese didn't care for religious subjects. What was being bought, said Freddie, were "these scribbles by Twombly," an action painter of the fifties; they were going for hundreds of thousands. This brought up other action painters; Arshile Gorky was mentioned. Freddie wondered if anybody had seen the nasty crack Gorky's daughter Maro had made about Muriel in a piece on the artists of the Chianti valley for *Harper's & Queen*, the October issue, he thought it was.

"What nasty crack?" asked Muriel, sharply on the alert. "What did she say about me?" But Freddie was mum. Only later, when I was in the sitting room and the others were in the kitchen preparing the coffee and Muriel was upstairs, did Penelope succeed in getting it out of Freddie that the nasty crack consisted of Maro Gorky's referring to Muriel as "that old crone in the red wig." At the dinner table, however, it was already clear that Muriel was furious: "She's never met me; I can't think what she can have to say about me." Penelope said, "She'd better watch out. Muriel may sue."

Earlier in the evening, Italy had been spared, but after the reference to Maro's "nasty crack," Muriel burst out, "I shall leave Tuscany; I will, if rude things are going to be said about me. I'll get right out."

Freddie tried to downplay what he now saw had been an indiscretion, and Dario denounced Maro as a hateful woman who was only being nasty because she couldn't stand it that she owed every little scrap of importance she could claim in the world to the fact that she had a famous father. But Muriel was not sidetracked. She went upstairs to her office to telephone Maro Gorky in an effort to confront her on the spot.

When Muriel came down into the kitchen, Penelope matter-of-factly reported what Freddie had been reluctant to say, that the crack was a reference to Muriel as "that old crone in a red wig," to which

Muriel cried, "I've never owned a wig. And I don't dye my hair red. What does she know about it anyway? She's never even met me!"

Once again, Freddie said he was sorry he'd ever brought it up.

We finally settled in the sitting room with coffee, and the conversation turned to other things. Still Muriel was glum. At one point she asked, quite out of the blue, if Maro had children, and being told she had "a boy and a girl," such a strange look came over her face that I feared for their well-being. I remembered that earlier, when Penelope, having opened the bottle, was just preparing to pour us all champagne, Muriel had said to the room at large, "Never pour with your left hand—it was the hand the Borgias used. They'd open the hinged ring they wore on the third finger of that hand, then turn the poison it contained into the vessel as they poured." She demonstrated neatly with a hinged ring of her own, and wound up, "So you must never pour left-handed."

I could easily imagine that had Maro Gorky been in the room at this moment, Muriel might have offered her a glass of champagne and poured it for her with her left hand.

It was just as well that Maro Gorky was not reachable that night. Freddie had not got his facts right. There was a nasty crack in *Harper's & Queen,* and it did occur in an article about Maro Gorky's rude luncheons and dinners for the English colony in the Chianti valley. But the author of the crack is described as a recently arrived man, a "high-pitched screamer" who was nowhere near as talented as Muriel, and the color of the wig was "orange."

At eleven the party broke up, all of us leaving together, Muriel and Penelope to see me home to Cortona, Freddie and Dario to repair to Freddie's house in Florence.

The traffic was heavy at first, then devolved to almost none when the driving became hazardous because of the fog. Both Penelope and Muriel insisted they didn't mind the lateness of the hour or the more than ninety miles of driving involved in getting me home and themselves back. I was originally to have stayed over, but they'd thought better of this plan, saying it was the scarcity of done-up rooms that posed a problem of where to put me. This was confirmed by the tour I'd been given as I arrived. I'd seen a small, peach-colored room that was Muriel's, and seen the studio couch/daybed in the library, where I was told Penelope slept. I'd even watched television in the one and dined in the other. But full of the aura of rather poisonous gossip Freddie had brought to the dinner table, and fed by a sense of disappointment, I allowed myself to wonder whether the real reason had been their reluctance to let me see that they shared a bed.

I began to let my imagination ride along with me on the trip back to Cortona. I imagined as more truth than exaggeration Muriel's humorous references to how Penny ordered her around, forcing her into slave labor in the olive grove attached to the church grounds each picking season. She also claimed she had been press-ganged into the work of redecorating the chapel, an area Penelope used as her studio. I found more evidence—of Penelope's devotion if not of her dominatrix tendencies—in the portrait she'd done of Muriel and wouldn't give her. On Muriel's side, I considered her preference for female company dating back to Miss Kay's class at James Gillespie's High School in Edinburgh (the model for Miss Brodie and her "set"). Then there were her difficulties with men: a husband who went off his rocker, and two lovers who delivered her literary stabs in the back. An Irish landlady of hers once observed, "You're a bad picker," and Muriel could only respond, "How true!" Add to this her predilection for women's clubs (chiefly one called the Helena, renamed the May of Teck in *The Girls of Slender Means*). And hadn't she also had a female flatmate for years in Rhodesia?

Unsurprisingly, there had been plenty of gossip about Muriel and Penelope's relationship.

Against these hints of full-blown passion between the two women were Muriel's repeated denials in print. "We're not lesbians, you know," she'd said in answering some impertinent interviewer. On another occasion she had described the relationship between her and Penelope as "old-fashioned friendship." Finally, I came to the conclusion that it was of no importance to anyone but them and none of my business. *Snap out of it*, I said to myself, *and pay attention so you can help with the driving.*

Penelope was being very offhand about the fog, though as an expert driver she was clearly concerned about it. At this point we could scarcely see the line in the center of the road. Suddenly she began to hum, rather loudly, a tune I recognized. Soon Muriel and I were humming, then lustily singing along. "By yon bonnie banks and by yon bonnie braes," we warbled.

I got out at my house a little before midnight. Watching the lights of the Alfa Romeo swing down the drive, I imagined first Penelope, then Muriel, breaking into song as they wound down to the valley floor, where the fog would envelop them once more.

But I am not satisfied to have this be the last glimpse I give of Muriel Spark. While this 1989 Christmas encounter in Tuscany brought out more of her sharper side, the luncheon we had together in Arezzo in 2004 made me aware once more of what a great soul she was. So lightly easy in her charity, in her generous treatment of me, her solicitude about my life and its twists and turns, as she became aware of them, in our infrequent exchanges of letters.

The last time we met she had to make a great effort to come all the way to Arezzo to accommodate a reunion with me on my brief sojourn in the area. By then she had turned eighty-four, and over the intervening years she had suffered hip and eye surgeries and a quantity of serious illnesses and flare-ups. But there she was, on a bright hot day in June, motoring with Penelope several tens of miles to treat me to lunch in the Hotel Minerva, where we were the only guests in the chandeliered grandeur of a great fancy dining room.

As if to justify all the expense—the waiting staff and the attentions of the maître d', the gilded trolleys of delicacies trotted out for her to select from—Muriel stood ready to, and did, order a great many more dishes and a great deal more vino, both *rosso* and *bianco,* than we could possibly eat or drink. Her condition rendered her able to partake only sparingly of any of it. Yet there she was, cheerfully inquiring after my welfare, my hopes, and my projects, and giving an enthusiastic account of her recent turn as a writer in residence at a private school somewhere, I thought she said, near the French-Swiss border. I felt certain she had taken the post not because she needed the money—though she always liked to add to her stash—but because she saw its potential as material for her work. Sure enough, her last novel, *The Finishing School,* takes place in just such a setting.

When we went to the car to part, she was ready with a warm embrace, a smile for the camera, and many expressions of affection. It was a fitting last memory that I am grateful for having gone to some trouble myself in order to achieve.

Soon after my return to America, the word came that Muriel

could not give me her response to my latest book because her sight had now entirely failed her. And then, on April 13, 2006, her life was over.

Penelope informed me that a memorial was being arranged in London for the following April. I asked my old friends from the Sussex Lifeboat Ball, Peter and Winifred Wroe, to attend in my stead. They described it as a wonderful concert in Wigmore Hall, well attended, consisting of beautiful music, exquisitely played, with not a somber note sounded.

Penelope wrote her appreciation for my attendance by proxy and said she had not yet been able to discipline herself to cheerfulness in a life without Muriel, describing herself as "like a child dragged kicking and screaming from the party, longing for more chocolate cake."

So there, in the Arezzo parking lot, fresh from pressing upon me a huge great slice of chocolate cake, is where I leave her. Good-bye, Muriel, and *grazie mille.*

Rough Passage through the *New Yorker* Art Department

Jack Kahn was mistaken when he said I'd never risen from my post as receptionist of the eighteenth floor. In April 1959, when I had been at *The New Yorker* for a year and a half, I was thrilled to be promoted to work as an assistant in the art department on twenty. As it turned out, I stayed there a mere six months, but the job had personal repercussions for me that nearly cost me my life.

Mailing out rejected cartoons in their own self-addressed stamped envelopes (SASEs) was one of my main tasks in my new position. I also assisted the director, James Geraghty, and his right-hand man, Don Hull. Don was responsible for a fast run-through of the unsolicited submissions, culling out the one in a million that might be bought. He liked to tell the story of the day, soon after he started in 1954, when the office was to undergo its first repainting ever, a new coat of the same noncommittal gray. In preparation for this event, the regulation steel desks were pulled into the center of the room awaiting a painter's drop cloth. Out tumbled thousands of eight-by-ten sheets of manila sketch paper of the kind most rough drawings were done on. They had been wedged into the perhaps three-and-a-half-inch gap between the desks and the walls, and they had been there for at least three years. Don speculated that they dated from the period in the early fifties when the twenty-three-year-old Truman Capote had spun his wheels in the art department as he waited for fame to come knocking at his door. Instead of going through the tedious process he'd been hired for, Truman had evidently been destroying the envelopes and dumping their contents behind whichever desk he was using at the time. For weeks and months, Don Hull had been left to placate the wailing, indignant callers whose drawings—forever separated from their SASEs—had been doomed to a nonresponse.

I could not help feeling a pang of sympathy as well as admiration for the ever-thwarted hopefuls whose work I was responsible for shuffling in and out of the slush pile. I tried to give them a week or two at least of hoping against hope before I dropped their efforts into return mail.

Almost as poignant for me was the knowledge that some measure of disappointment awaited the fifteen or twenty *New Yorker* artists who came in weekly to learn the fate of their last week's submissions. Art director James Geraghty, editor William Shawn, and layout chief Carmine Peppe met every Monday and went over the roughs (preliminary sketches) supplied by the regular contributors. It would be their thumbs-up or -down that would set the mood, merry or glum, among the Tuesday lunchers with Geraghty or the Wednesday lunchers with Geraghty's surrogate, Frank Modell, a cartoonist himself.

A year or so ago, *The New York Times* ran a feature in its Sunday City section on the Tuesday lunches ritually engaged in by the *New Yorker* cartoonists. The names and faces were different and the restaurant was different, but the sense of crisis underlying the superficially casual air at the lunch table was the same—the undercurrent of nervous energy as each ego put itself on the line to amuse, or fail to amuse. Each career fluttered in the uptick of a sale or the downtick of a rejection or, more commonly, a mix of the two.

All just the same.

Small wonder that they were, in the main, a restive bunch. Short on self-confidence, long on nervous laughter.

The atmosphere in the anteroom of Mr. Geraghty's office on Tuesdays matched the descriptions Woody Allen, Carl Reiner, and others have given of the gag writer's room at NBC when preparing for Sid Caesar's *Caesar's Hour,* a sixty-minute show produced weekly in the 1950s before a live audience. It was the atmosphere reflected in the 1982 film about those comedy shows, *My Favorite Year,* with Peter O'Toole. The recent NBC drama *Studio 60 on the Sunset Strip,* too, attempted to capture the seriously funny panic reactions induced while providing amusement on demand—giddiness, nausea, head banging, and crying jags being about the usual range. There is a lot of throwing up involved in comedy, it seems.

After seeing a favored few artists in private audience each Tuesday, Jim G. would come striding out of his office, ready to pretend that he and all those he'd left cooling their heels in the anteroom would enjoy the forthcoming lunch in a spirit of undiluted bonhomie. Helen Hokinson being dead and Roz Chast yet to come onboard, all of those attending were men, and most were hefting the considerable burdens of a house and a family in Connecticut. Trying to be funny with bill collectors in the wings often placed superhuman demands upon the human psyche.

Up close as I was for those six months in the art department, I never quite got over the sense that I was among the walking wounded. I came to understand that the various remedies of drink, nicotine, and other pain-deadening drugs were being consumed by these artists more in a medicinal than a Rabelaisian spirit. Their doctors, if not they, were convinced that they needed the dosages administered simply to hold these delicate plants together. Tremors of limbs born of too much—or too little—alcohol; slouches; and vacant stares should the plant be over- (or under-) medicated were, I learned, pretty much the norm. One way or another, the *New Yorker* artists all bore witness to the strain on the human body that creative types undergo. No matter how hard I laughed, how much I admired, how I sympathized, I could never forget or ignore the pain. Maybe it was just a variation on the pain of Everyman, but in my eyes it gave those funny men a heroic patina that intensified the moments I spent in their company.

Of course, I now see that this excess of fellow feeling for the artists was exactly what scuttled my chances of making a go of it there. My predecessor, a woman I shall call Brenda, who had been Jim Geraghty's most successful assistant in the past, set the mold. British wit, a hint of military spit and polish, razor-tongued ripostes, and pull-up-your-socks dismissals were that slender lady's hallmark. She thought nothing of going to bed with the boss, bullying him for money to buy a new winter coat, or bandying insults and wisecracks with the boys while turning a deaf ear to their pleas for second looks at this week's roughs.

The previous winter, Brenda had gone skiing in Gstaad with a married banker, also a Brit. Discovering that she preferred the banker and the skiing in Gstaad to the care and feeding of *New Yorker* cartoonists, she wired that come April she would no longer be at her desk. And so I was brought in to fill the job. But where

Brenda was hard, I was soft; where she was ruthless, I was wimpy; where she was what Jim Geraghty wanted, I was unquestionably not. So when, after six months, I had the poor judgment to take my first vacation—a month's grand tour of Europe—I was ambushed. I came back to find a beaming Mr. Geraghty asking if I did not think it "super" that Brenda had changed her mind about joining the jet set. She was reclaiming her old post, while I was to be sent back down to the eighteenth floor where I'd come from. This proved to be nothing more than a well-intentioned ruse. Brenda soon decamped for Portillo, and another girl was quietly brought in.

That I didn't see this coming shows how little I understood about the workings of power on any level. Oh, I knew that Mr. Geraghty and I were not warming to each other (he remained Mr. Geraghty throughout our association), but I certainly had no clue that that was the whole ball game. While failing miserably to win the favor of my boss, I was made something of a pet by the artists. Frank Modell, a noted ladies' man, took me to lunch at Del Pezzo's and seemed content to be the affable cheerleader of my love life. Warren Miller and William Steig, on a postprandial stroll through the Village, were tickled to learn that my pals and I at the University of Minnesota used to serve drinks on Steig napkins captioned "People are no damned good." Anatol Kovarsky, a cover artist, spent a chummy evening with me in Washington Square taking in a chamber concert, and Arthur Getz hired me to sit for him for some paintings he was doing for a gallery show. I later turned up on one of his covers. I was the girl with her hair up and her topknot surrounded by fake pearls in the box office of a movie theater—which delighted my pop, for we used to own and operate a movie house.

Mr. Getz was wonderful during those posing sessions. Very patient and professional, he insisted that I use his box-seat ticket for *Giselle,* being danced by the Royal Ballet at the Met the very day of our last sit. He was going to stay on at his studio and finish the picture we had begun together. When the end came, he alone of all the artists wrote me a note saying he was sorry things had not turned out better for me.

Little did Arthur Getz or Geraghty or any of them know just how badly they had turned out. It was not until much later in my tenure at *The New Yorker* that a bright summer intern from Smith College brought me face-to-face with a chapter in my history over which I had drawn a veil. The period I had chosen to forget was 1959–1960, round about the time I was sent back in dudgeon from the art department to my receptionist's chair. The Smithie, Ivy Eberhart by name, who covered for me on my lunch hours, adopted me as a kind of mentor. One afternoon, in 1972, she hovered at my desk, clearly wishing to ask me something. "Do you by any chance know a cartoonist named Evan Simm? Because he has been asking me out and I think I have made a foolish mistake in saying yes on several occasions." Thus, innocently, did Ivy become the cracker of my memory vault. I think all I said to her at the time was something like, "Yes, I do know him, and my advice to you is to have as little as possible to do with him. He's bad news."

The bearer of this "bad news" rubric, whom I am calling Evan Simm, was still a young man at the time I first knew him, and one of the lucky few to make it into the Wednesday art meetings. Evan lived the life of a man on a tightrope, dependent from week to week on the all-important meeting. Would one of his roughs be chosen for a finished cartoon? Would he be given an "idea," at least? Some of the artists on drawing accounts who were better draftsmen than hatchers of jokes would be given ideas to finish that had come in over the transom, the freelance gag writers getting fifty dollars per idea used. There were a few artists in the top tier—Charles Addams and Peter Arno, for example—who were regularly given "Addams" or "Arno" ideas to finish. In Charles Addams's case, they would feature Gothic mansions or graveyards; in Peter Arno's, leather banquettes at the Copa with sugar daddies and showgirls in the foreground. Such settings and the humor that went with them were by this time so associated in the public mind with these men that freelancers often cooked up ideas especially for them.

Most regulars, however, did their own ideas the majority of the time. (It called for a combination of talents rather like those of a composer-lyricist, and it was the rarities, like Cole Porter and Irving Berlin, who managed to be equally prolific at both.) Artists who, like Evan, never stopped trying to be both gag writer and draftsman continued to struggle more or less unsuccessfully to get OKs for their roughs, with their own captions attached, if captions were called for. Such artists were acknowledged to have mastered distinctive drawing styles, producing drawings on a regular basis that "looked right" in the magazine, but they often came to the art gatherings with chips on their shoulders, feeling like second stringers who never got to the plate often enough. Evan was one of these.

At twenty-eight, he was one of the youngest of the Wednesday regulars. He was a midwesterner who had come east for college. His father held a wartime post in Washington, DC, and Evan, so as not to disrupt his schooling, remained for the duration at home with his mother in Elgin, Illinois. Perhaps because of this, Evan had conceived a yearning for the tonier East. In any case, he got his BA in art at Cornell. Every young man had two years of military service to perform in those years, and Evan chose to do his as an enlistee in the army, where, at his request, he was posted to Japan.

For an artist, this was a good fit, a rare instance of the army getting the right man in the right place at the right time. Whenever Evan was not drawing for *Stars and Stripes*—in other words, whenever he was free to leave the base—he spent his time living like a native in a rice-paper house with a Japanese girlfriend. He was quickly absorbed into Japanese life, learning a bit of the language and, as much as a Westerner could, embracing the Japanese sensibility. He loved the food, the beer, the sake, the chopsticks, the shoji screens, the art of bonsai, the game of Go, the novels of Kobo Abe, the films of Akira Kurosawa, the sculptures of Isamu Noguchi. When his hitch was up, he elected to stay on, getting a job as a draftsman in the publicity office of an international company. There, he met a young Austrian woman, Marta, who shared his enthusiasm for all things Japanese.

The boyhood and adolescence Evan had gone through in Elgin had in many ways sapped his confidence. He was unathletic. He had a kind of awkward, shambling gait. His looks were unprepossessing. His skin was clear, and although his hair was a pleasant honey color in summer and light brown in winter, it lay limp and straight and flopped onto his brow. Nevertheless, he let it grow out of its military buzz cut as soon as he was discharged. He dressed in kimono-like coats when in Japan and continued to dress in soft cotton materials when he went west. He had a wardrobe filled with clean, soft, attractive, and comfortable casual clothes—white button-down shirts or blue cotton work shirts, worn with pressed chinos and deerskin boots. So his skin, hair, and clothes were not the problem. The problem was his face.

His features were of a comic lumpiness. He had a jug chin, a knobby nose, and a pair of blue eyes that looked too close together and tended to disappear under light brows and lashes that did nothing to mitigate the rest. It was a face that invited teasing on the playground, on the gym floor, and on the parade ground. Evan knew by the time he was thirteen that he was never going to be taken seriously. So, like Lou Costello, Buddy Hackett, and other non-Adonises before him, he decided to protect himself by making the jokes before the other guys got around to it. That defense mechanism got him through the minefield of junior and senior high, but college was tougher. He lost valuable support on account of his father's long periods away from home. Evan worshipped the guy, but his father seemed happy to do anything and be anywhere but home. Evan's mother may have been the root cause of this reluctance. She was a mousy-looking woman, and very weird socially.

All this made it hard for Evan to find himself as a man, and easy for him to be resentful and somewhat suspicious of the female of the species. But the army worked wonders in forcing upon him a certain amount of male bonding, and Japanese women did the rest. He came out of his tour in Tokyo with confidence in himself, both as a man who could fend for himself in a man's world, and as a guy who could go after, and get, the prettiest women he met, from the East or the West.

One of Evan's chief strategies for coping came from listening to his father's lessons on how to manipulate people. As a propaganda officer, the senior Simm put together war-bond drives; pro-American, anti-Nazi scripts for Hollywood films; slogans; posters; and patriotic campaigns of all kinds, designed to sway public opinion, elevate public morale, and keep enthusiasm and support for the war effort at an optimum level. Evan listened with fascination to all this—on his dad's precious sojourns at home—and picked up tips that he found useful when laying siege to a young woman's defenses.

Evan was a realist. He knew that number two would have to try harder. Aggressive courtship was his answer to the glamour boys whose more obvious physical appeal led them barely to exert themselves, knowing that, without their lifting a finger, women would fall all over them. He followed the first request for a date—nearly always refused—with a barrage of requests, until a yes was secured. He then made it his business to come up with interesting places to go and indulge a gift for openhanded expenditure—on food, booze, music, and culture. Excellent entertainment became the signature of an Evan Simm courtship. Evan in full swing seldom left the object of his desire unmoved or unconquered.

So it was with the popular and vivacious Marta. She was slender, long waisted, even featured, and bright eyed and had a shaft of swinging chestnut hair, a package that was accompanied by swaying hips, a flirtatious smile, charmingly accented English, and a manner that manifested plenty of confidence in all these attributes. Marta was every bit as experienced and sophisticated sexually as Evan and would often slip out of his clutches and into the arms of a waiting Eurasian, European, or Japanese rival if Evan did not work ceaselessly at commandeering her time. She became, finally, a prize he felt he must claim. And so, before her international job assignment in Japan came to an end, he bought an emerald ring (both thought diamonds too clichéd) and dropped to one knee in the classic mode of the marriage proposal. Somehow the ring got accepted before the proposal. It seemed there were going to be conditions that might take weeks, even months, to meet. Marta would need to return to Austria, her native land, make arrangements to get her travel papers in order, pay a long-promised six-month visit to her mother. Then, and only then, would she be ready to join Evan as his betrothed.

In 1958, Evan reentered the United States, where *The New Yorker* had, on the strength of the drawings he'd been submitting—and, increasingly, selling—over the previous year, offered him a starter contract. He began attending weekly art gatherings and took a rent-controlled fourth-floor walk-up in the rear of a building near the corner of West Fourth and Bank Streets. He had a lothario of a landlord, Al, whom he idealized and who would come to play a major role in my own life. But I'm getting ahead of myself. Old brownstones lined the streets, and spindly, wire-protected, yet peed-upon ailanthus trees shaded the brownstones. Treasured by the residents were backyards full of gardens, koi ponds, cobblestone paths, bamboo fences, barbecue pits, and little French bistro tables. Evan's place on the top floor overlooked this pleasant panorama. From a minuscule front hall, it went two steps up to a small library fitted only with a German metal swing lamp and a beanbag chair; the floor-to-ceiling bookcases, filled with a large collection of art books, ran the length of the apartment. The other wall was left with its bricks exposed. Up another step was the bedroom, or, rather, a Japanese open-box canopy frame above a platform bed that made a kind of room of its own.

Evan, dressed in a navy-and-white kimono, listening to Count

Basie's "Li'l Darlin'," Billie Holiday, and other jazz records on his Bang and Olufsen turntable, was to all outward appearances at home with the condition of bachelorhood. However, as the days and weeks of his separation from Marta stretched on, he began to cast about for a replacement.

This is where I come in.

My affair with Evan Simm began in late spring of 1959 and lasted for less than a year.

We had been seeing each other for several weeks—a lunch, two dinners, and a movie—when Evan said, "Come up to my place for dinner and I'll show you my Japanese prints." The joke was he wasn't kidding.

I walked up to his fourth-floor apartment at 7:30 p.m, on a mild, seventy-degree evening in June. After a good look at his book of Arno drawings and, yes, some Japanese prints, we moved for a second round of Tanqueray martinis to the back porch, where night had fallen; lights were flickering in the buildings across the way, and paper lanterns swung and glowed in the gardens below. Evan prepared two T-bones, medium rare, over a charcoal-burning hibachi, and pulled out of the refrigerator two green salads, which he tossed lightly with vinegar and oil. I put candles inside the hurricane shades and lit them and we settled down to some serious eating. Fred Astaire sang "They Can't Take That Away from Me," accompanied by Oscar Peterson. I remember Evan's saying as we touched glasses, "Here's to the beautiful children we'll have together."

The apartment, the dinner, the cocktails, the love songs, the reference to what beautiful children I could give him, all signified to me, in my misreading of the code we were following, that it was a serious relationship we were about to enter, one that justified the surrender of my hitherto carefully guarded virginity. Soon we were naked on top of one another, in the candlelit confines of Evan's platform bed, where he tenderly discovered and then set about physically confirming the virginal state of my body. I rode through the experience as if borne along on an ocean wave, taking in the surprising gentleness of Evan's lovemaking, and appreciating to the depths of my English-major soul the compliment he paid my breasts: "They look like the faces of two young perch." To my trusting mind, all of this was following a classic pattern. I knew—or thought I knew—that these references to children and this biblical flattery were oblique allusions to a forthcoming proposal of marriage. As a practiced hand at this sort of thing, Evan knew better.

The follow-up was equally irresistible. I was delivered home at sunrise, and after I had slept only a few hours, two dozen long-stemmed red roses—the first ever in my date book—were delivered to my door, impressing the hell out of my British roommate.

It must have been about noon the "morning after." I had just finished trimming the stems and arranging the roses when Evan called and said he would be picking me up in half an hour. He said he owned a cunning orange Volkswagen and we were going to take a little trip in it to Lancaster County—Pennsylvania Dutch territory in the Brandywine Valley. I put on a black cotton dress, with a wide, swinging skirt and bright pink sprigs of dogwood on it, and some strappy raffia sandals, and by the time I had packed a big straw bag to sling over my shoulder, the buzzer told me he was at the door.

So began a surreal thirty-six hours during which Evan kept up a steady stream of chatter regarding the delights, cultural, ethnic, equine, gustatorial, and architectural, of the terrain toward which we were headed.

We stopped midafternoon in a little tea shop on the outskirts of Amish country, and I had my first mint julep, in a frosty silver tankard with a fresh mint leaf sticking out of the top. All very heady, but my excitement was somewhat tempered by concerns that there was something wrong; I had needed a sanitary pad to stanch bleeding I had no clue about the significance of. Was I damaged goods in some literal sense? Was I jeopardizing my ability to have those "beautiful children" Evan had so seductively dangled before my eyes the night before? Ought I to be recovering from this earthshaking change in my body by twenty-four hours of bed rest in a darkened room instead of swanning about the countryside with cocktail stops on the itinerary?

If I spoke at all, God knows what I said. Certainly nothing to the point. Meanwhile, Evan solicitously plied me with BLTs and a roster of local pleasures that included quilt shops and the Andrew Wyeth gallery. As I was to learn, he never failed to pursue a piece of art or sculpture he admired, and the hyperrealism of the Wyeth country scenes touched that area of his aesthetic makeup that he had so fully developed in Japan.

In the late afternoon we drew up to a parking lot outside the Lancaster County Fair. Evan exclaimed with pleasure at an advertising bill announcing a stage show appearance later that evening by Anna Russell, a singer from New South Wales who made fun of opera. Her condensed account of *The Ring of the Niebelung,* Evan assured me, would have me in stitches. He bought tickets, and fortified with further drinks (no more juleps, but gin and tonics, as I recall), we did indeed laugh lustily at Miss Russell, a buxom woman in her fifties, who played the appreciative crowd like a maestro, polishing us off with a second of her famous set pieces, "How to Write Your Own Gilbert and Sullivan Opera."

Did I worry about where I would lay my fuzzy blond head that night? What, *me* worry? I was in no state to ponder the sexual mechanics of lovemaking through Kotexes or to go in for woozy wonderings about my moral condition. Was I a young woman no longer a maiden but still respectable? Or was my moral condition conditional upon my being—or not being—engaged to be married? We stayed, as I recall, in a twee bed-and-breakfast with such a quantity of mattress and bedding that I forgot whether any of it turned pink during the night's amours. A breakfast of popovers was still being served as we exited around noon the Sunday of this extraordinary trio of days.

Was ever a seduction so drawn out and so hedged about with museum viewings, green fields, and fresh garden-grown salads? I was deposited back at my West Seventy-Fifth Street lodgings sometime after midnight, none the wiser, though maybe an indefinable bit sadder than when I had left them.

My roommate's head was deep in her pillow on the parlor couch. She had not taken the cover off my bed. I suppose she was convinced by this time that I had gone for the duration of the weekend, if not permanently decamped.

My head did begin to clear after stumbling into the office at ten on Monday morning, glad of *The New Yorker*'s staggered office hours. But somehow I never did take myself in hand for an examination of my own actions. I thought at the time that it was because I was so fascinated to see what new act of extravagant courtship Evan would come up with. I now think I was so alienated from my own feelings as to have—in the emotional sense—none. Physically, I soon grew out of that initial state of stiffness and soreness, awakening to an entirely new erotic bliss that was as much due to a native "taking to it" on my part, which surprised us both, as to the expertise of my lover. Whenever I was not actually in bed with Evan in those first weeks of summer 1959, I was dreamily contemplating being in bed with him. It was a whole new world, all right.

Throughout June, July, and August, Evan suggested with gratifying regularity that we lunch together as well as breakfast and dine together. And he seemed to know a bewildering array of Midtown restaurants. The two or three specializing in Japanese cuisine were high on his list. He waxed so mystically eloquent about the Japanese broth called miso that I believed I liked it. Similarly, the delights of tempura and dipped sweet potato or turnip and a variety of cold noodles. Fumbling with chopsticks and sitting cross-legged on mats became for me, if not poised accomplishments, at least no longer occasions for general hilarity.

Our nighttime entertainments were dim-lit cocktail lounges all over town. One bar on Fifty-Seventh Street, called the Menemsha, was famous for its feature of a not very convincing storm. The room was lined on three sides with sailing-ship dioramas. Every forty minutes or so, the lights would dim, followed by bursts of lightning, claps of thunder, and dangerously rocking tanks full of water, which required all gentlemen present to put their arms around their ladies for safety. As if a tankful of water could—even by bursting—put us at hazard. Every woman in the room played along. Pretty clever, the restaurateur who thought that one up.

We checked out Chumley's and the Cedar and the King Cole and Bemelmans and pretty much all the best-known bars in the city. Dinner, when not Japanese, was often at some other cozy little ethnic restaurant up or down Second Avenue. I began to realize that Evan was spending an awful lot of money, for although the places we ate might have been relatively modest, the habits that we indulged were expensive—cover charges and high-priced drinks at every jazz spot in town. We saw and heard Stan Getz and Anita O'Day. We caught Nina Simone at the Village Vanguard, Maynard Ferguson at Birdland, Roy Eldridge at Jimmy Ryan's, and Bobby Hackett at Eddie Condon's. The *New Yorker* cartoonist Lee Lorenz played every Monday down at Marie's Crisis Café, and we often went down to see him at the bar where Thomas Paine wrote a series of his most inflammatory tracts, called "The American Crisis," at the window table in the front. We also saw on several memorable occasions at Marie's a wonderful tap dancer called John Bubbles.

But the place we came back to again and again was the Five Spot in the East Village, to hear Thelonious Monk in what must have been a summer-long gig. Here my education in the stratosphere of jazz piano became complete. The room was always covered in a blue haze of smoke; the crowd was always putting away quantities of scotch. Dewar's and soda became my drink for its ability to build to a not incapacitating buzz that could be sustained through the four or five drinks that Evan consumed during an average stay. Was I listening? he'd ask. Did I hear that? Did I follow what sophisticated variations the Monk was pulling out of the long-since-abandoned melody? Yes, I was listening. Yes, I heard, and yes, I was caught up in the sense of a musician far, far away inside his own head; but truth to tell, I have never been able to keep hold of a melodic line past the third or fourth variation, and the atonal stuff left me completely at a loss. Never mind, Evan liked it and I was there to learn.

When I got back from the grand tour that separated me from Evan for nearly four weeks—and me from the *New Yorker* art department forever—it was immediately apparent that something had shifted. Mainly him. He had become shifty eyed. This was unnecessary, since he had seen this coming all along, but perhaps it made him nervous that I had been a virgin. He was used to more experienced partners who were better at the game. He began using a cutting style of mockery, making fun of what he called my "Aw, shucks" manner and attributing it to my "Spamtown upbringing." I couldn't seem to stop hunting for relationship clues. Were we engaged or weren't we? And why, each time I attempted clarification, did Evan turn so mean?

On the first of October, at Evan's suggestion, I moved down to Jane Street in Greenwich Village to an apartment with no roommate. He said it was more convenient. The places we went to in October were basically the same places we had gone to all summer, but their importance as glamorous lead-ups to bed now seemed a bit threadbare and transparent.

In early November I was heartened when Evan asked me to arrange a long lunch hour in order to view an apartment he wanted me to see, which was for rent and immediate occupancy, on Washington Square. We were welcomed into the bare flat by the landlady, a bright-eyed woman with a curly frizz of salt-and-pepper hair, the leathery, wrinkled skin of a heavy smoker, and the determinedly cheerful demeanor of the businesswoman ready to close a deal.

After she finished showing us through the somewhat dim one-bedroom apartment on the second-floor front of the old brownstone (a matter of a very few minutes), Evan invited me to give him my opinion.

"Well," I began dubiously, as I peered into the shallow hall cubbyhole that separated the front parlor from the rear bedroom, a hall that also contained what there was of a Pullman kitchen and a bathroom with a two-foot-square shower stall and no tub. "There isn't much closet space." "Oh"—the landlady shrugged, jiggling her ring of keys—"putting one of those charming French armoires in the bedroom will take care of that." Perhaps realizing that she needed to do more in order to enlist me on her side, she gave me a toothy smile and said, "It is so good of you, dear, to come down here with Mr. Simm on your lunch hour to give him, as he put it to me, 'the woman's point of view.'" Shifting her smile to "Mr. Simm," she went on, "When was it you said your fiancée would be coming over from Austria? December? I wish I could hold it for that long, but as I mentioned on the phone, I have another party waiting, and if I am to keep it for you, I really have to have a deposit today."

Evan took my elbow and drew me into the comparative privacy of the bedroom, where he must have been moved by the stricken look on my face as I hissed, "Fiancée? Fiancée?" All he could do was mumble, with a rueful grin, "Oh, what tangled webs we weave, when first we practice to deceive." I remember thinking, even through the yellowish blue of pain closing down over my eyes and forehead, that it was unbelievable that he could be both so apt and so literary at such a moment.

How I got through the rest of that day, how I got back to the office, took up my chair at my desk, endured the routine of the remaining four hours of the workday, I haven't a clue—all passed without leaving a trace in my memory.

In December, Evan married.

In January he called and I let him back into my apartment and back into my bed. The rest of that month found me ignorant as ever of my own inner life, yet exploring depths of self-loathing and self-revulsion I hadn't known existed.

I see that in giving my account of this affair, I have told nothing about my own feelings. Was I even in love with this man I was condemning for having falsely avowed love for me—perhaps without feeling a trace of love for him? I thrilled to his touch—did that mean I was attracted to him physically but not morally or spiritually? Truth to tell, I was not attracted to him at all except as a torso, with legs and a penis of fine proportions. I thought he was funny looking, jug jawed and knobby nosed and ungraceful in stride. How in the world, if I was not attracted to him, did it happen that I thrilled to his touch? Quite surprisingly, these were questions I did not ask.

I did, however, begin keeping notebooks.

> Now I am lost. I'm not even sure of my sex any longer. I want to swing from the rafters, to hurl a bottle of ink at a white wall. I loathe that I haven't the courage to do either of those things. I haven't the courage to walk into the water as Virginia Woolf did. She weighted her pockets. I would not find it necessary—I can't swim.
>
> Cover up. Hold tight. Shut up and wait. That's what I do. But lately I know it is wrong and dangerous. I've begun to shout. The wrong words at the wrong people. All the louder because I did not do it when I should have.

But for those notebook entries I might have remained clueless about what was happening to me and thus escaped harm altogether. Yet there was the abyss, waiting to stare me in the face when, on Wednesday, February 3, I narrowly avoided desecrating Evan and Marta's marriage bed. Evan had insisted we stop at the Ninth Street digs he and Marta had moved into to pick up his "forgotten wallet." Marta was in St. Vincent's, where she had been hospitalized with appendicitis. When I refused the offered bed (offered to my horror), Evan accompanied me in a taxi to my place and left me at the curb. Not because his finer feelings surfaced, but because he had to go and fetch Marta, and as he explained to me, my push-back at Ninth Street had cost us valuable adultery time. I got up to my cold, high-ceilinged flat with no conscious participation of my own. *Yes,* I thought as I opened the door, *this is hell. This is where I live now.*

That evening I attempted suicide. My life, as I learned later on, had hinged upon a misunderstanding. I knew you were supposed to stuff a rug under the door when gassing yourself. But not having any rugs, I took at face value the notice on my aluminum-plated front door proclaiming it a fire door. Assuming that this meant it was airtight, I blew out the pilot light, turned on the oven, opened all the burners, and went to bed.

I was slapped back into groggy consciousness to find an oxygen mask over my mouth, an intern shaking me, the lights, the damned lights, blazing, the doors and windows wide open, and a mortifying cluster of neighbors and policemen around my bed. The neighbors I could hardly resent. It was their home I had nearly destroyed. True, I had thought the house was empty at the time, but I had given no thought to the inflammatory possibilities of a house with a serious gas leak. Dimly I was aware of Art, the neighbor from downstairs, telling the policeman how lucky it was that he and his wife had decided to come back from their country place early, and how he had gotten in by climbing the fire escape and jimmying the badly warped sash on my fire escape window.

Later, in the ambulance, I noticed the intern's hairy arms as he pressed me close to his starched white jacket, and I saw that he had a nice face as he looked into mine and said something like, "Oh, sweetheart, what have you done? And why have you done it?"

The attendant at Bellevue was much less attractive and not at all nice. She said two things only, "Strip," and "Shower with this bar of disinfectant." After that, she handed me a blue two-piece pajama suit and a pair of paper slippers.

The women's dorm was fairly quiet, if you didn't count snores, but the likelihood of sleep was sharply reduced by the bare bulbs burning on through what seemed like twelve hours of the night. But that couldn't have been true, because at 7:00 a.m. we were lined up and taken to a dining hall and given oatmeal and weak coffee—in other words, breakfast.

Dr. Feingold told me, when he saw me sometime later that day, that he was recommending a week of observation, after which, if another evaluation merited release, I would be given the name of a short-term therapist to whom weekly visits would be prescribed.

"I spoke to your parents," he said.

I opened my eyes wide at that.

"Your mother came on the line. I told her I was a doctor calling from a hospital in New York. I heard your father's voice in the background asking, 'Is she pregnant?' I assured your mother that you were not pregnant and that you were all right."

"What did you say had happened?" I asked around stiff lips.

"Only that you had been brought in because you had tried to hurt yourself a little."

"Oh, great," I replied.

Dr. Feingold seemed very young. A resident psychiatrist probably, sympathetic, but he clearly didn't have a clue about how to dispel alarm in middle-class parents standing in the kitchen of the living quarters behind their mom-and-pop grocery, trying to make a go of it out in southern Minnesota.

When I could have visitors, my pal Lizzie came around with a book and a magazine I had requested and asked, "What in the hell are you doing here?"

My office mate Betts was too polite to say the same, but I could see that she was just as mystified.

Later that week, a second evaluation resulted in my release from Bellevue, though there was good reason to suppose I was still in deep trouble. On the slender excuse that I knew no one else with a car, I called Evan and asked him to pick me up. What was I thinking? He agreed. He always knew good eating places, and it being noonish, he took us to a fifties diner on First Avenue that still had jukeboxes. Over tuna sandwiches he let me choose and I chose the song with the lyric "You must remember this," and Evan said, "Yes, there is such comfort in cheap music, isn't there?" That, finally, did it. I was still too sick in the head to muster anger at his miserable behavior toward me, but Evan's misquote of Noel Coward put an end once and for all to my sleeping with him. How could I ever go to bed with someone who not only misquoted Coward but could dis the song Ingrid was humming just before she said, "Play it, Sam"?

As for the rest of Evan Simm's story, it was so full of madness, sickness, and death as to evoke pity even in me. He used the imminent arrival of his child to order a lot of custom cabinetry to be installed in his two-bedroom flat on Ninth Street. Custom cabinetry is expensive, and Evan exerted a lot of pressure on Jim Geraghty to give him a drawing account and office space at the magazine. This would have to be on the eighteenth floor (*my* floor), an area mainly given over to writers, two departments (fashion and Talk), the mail room, and the library. Only six other cartoonists had offices there: Charles Addams, Frank Modell, James Stevenson, Ed Koren, Bob Weber, and Warren Miller. Perhaps detecting a look of desperation in Evan's eye, Geraghty gave in. The move did not, however, result in more purchases of Simm cartoons. As his drawing account grew, Evan's troubles grew, too. The baby arrived. When the little girl was no more than two, Marta was hospitalized for what may have been bipolar disorder. Evan sent for his mother to look after the child. A little woman, uncertain on her pins, she made a dazed trip or two through the eighteenth floor to her son's office, perhaps in search of an emergency set of keys, or cab fare.

Hardly a faithful husband, and now with no wife at home to be faithful to, Evan's pattern of too many girls, too much drinking, too much nightlife, and too many unpaid bills went into high gear. He grew a beard, which somewhat improved his jug chin by hiding its outline but emphasized his nose in an unfortunate way. The drinking was giving it the telltale flush of pink that comes of tiny burst blood vessels and has been seen in drinkers' noses ever since W. C. Fields—maybe ever since Bacchus.

I was forced to see him slouching past my desk daily. I did my best to ignore him or, failing that, gave him censorious looks. When he got to the office before me, he took to leaving me message-pad drawings designed to soften the unsoftenable. Day after day I would come in and there would be another variation on the theme of the punning soup series. The constant was a shallow bowl of soup with a spoon resting beside the full-to-the-brim, steaming vessel. Some of the variations: A turtle's head would emerge from the center of the bowl, looking sick and holding a partially smoked cigar. A caption on the back would read, "Green turtle." A ropy, hairy appendage with longer black hairs at the end would droop bowlside and be labeled "Oxtail." The head of a wattled, becombed chicken would occupy center bowl and be dubbed "Chicken noodle." On and on it went, going through ever more groan-inducing puns until a blond nude lifted her saucy torso from the midst of a number called "Wanton."

It all seemed too little and too late to me, a mere Band-Aid applied to a broken heart that didn't begin to salve my wounds. But what did I know? Hadn't someone named Norman Lear or Norman Jewison—anyway, Norman something—written a book that year about how watching Groucho Marx movies had cured him of cancer? So for all I knew, these stupid cartoons were playing their part in healing me. At any rate, Evan's amusing drawings did me no harm, and I now think they came from his hands as a rather touchingly inhibited stab at an apology, a mea culpa in cartoons.

Meanwhile, the slide of Evan's career at the magazine continued. I could see how completely it was in eclipse by the look of amused disgust with which Ivy told of his having "practically ordered" her to have drinks with him—"twice!" Her tales of nightmarish scenes of too many martinis, weavings into and out of cabs, and narrow escapes from his clutches, at the Algonquin and afterward, made it only too apparent.

Finally, when the strain Evan put on his drawing account burst even *The New Yorker*'s generous bounds, he was asked to vacate the premises. For several tipsy days he continued, defiantly, to come in, but under a court order, he ceased doing even that. A moving company packed his belongings and shipped them to him. Painters came in with fresh white paint, and within a week, it was as if Evan Simm had never been. His career at the magazine over, a large part of his life must have ended with it. He labored on, one doesn't know how, until 2004, when Cornell announced his name on its annual list of alumni deaths.

I now see that my conviction, during my affair with Evan, that I was in a preengagement phase of a relationship that was leading inevitably to marriage, children, and a station wagon in Connecticut was an illusion. Nor am I so deluded as to imagine I ever truly loved Evan. What caused searing pains to shoot from my chest through my head and made me come home nights and fall, scotch bottle in hand, into a butterfly chair dyed a revolting shade of bright terracotta was the sense that I had become part of a dumb blond cliché. Phrases like *fallen woman, seduced and abandoned, damaged goods, no respect in the morning,* all the tired claptrap of the worst scenarios of the cheapest novels and grade-B Hollywood pictures, tormented me. Had I been privy to just a little more perspective, I would have recognized it as the stuff of much better literature and music as well: of *Les liaisons dangereuses, Tess of the Durbervilles,* fully half of the best blues songs ever written, many a grand opera, and many a fine play (including a couple by William Shakespeare, though he usually fixed his up with a wedding in act 5). Even so, if I had realized sooner that what was injured in me by Evan's treachery was not my heart but a totally immature girl's vanity, it might have stung a good deal less, and I would have been much less likely to spin myself into the spiral of promiscuity that followed.

Party Girl

Beginning with my discovery of Evan's betrayal in November 1959 and lasting well beyond Easter into May 1960, my love life became a disaster area. This only exacerbated my self-hatred, which reached new heights—no, depths—after Evan. What does the disintegrating self look like? In my case, it looked a lot like fun. If only the self-condemnation could have been severed from the deed.

A degrading pattern emerged: a round of partying, always ending in the same way, a drink too far, a one-night stand. Then, dismaying me further, a growing list of my onetime sex partners came back for more, going so far as to precede mattress acrobatics with dinner and a show. In other words, they liked me better than I thought they should.

No longer able to consider myself a credible ingenue (is that polite stagespeak for *virgin*?), or at any rate an inexperienced naïf, I began acting out the role of the party girl/woman of the world. One of the props I added was the short amber cigarette holder I acquired in Europe, using it as a filter between me and the unfiltered Pall Malls I favored—the very prop Professor Morgan Blum accused me of *writing* with when he read my first attempt at a novel. I kept the Pall Malls in an Italian leather case and lit them with a silver propane lighter acquired in Europe, too, courtesy of my sophisticator in chief, Frank Cucci.

I met Frank before my discovery of Evan's treachery, even before I moved up to the art department, but in my new world-weary guise, I was able to draw on much that I learned under his tutelage. A more finely featured version of Frankie Avalon, with a brand-new Harvard degree in comparative lit, Frank was whiling away the time as he waited for his mandatory two years in the service to begin—he'd asked for an army posting to either Germany or the Far East. So he took a menial job in the mail room at *The New Yorker*, an amusing item, he figured, on the jacket copy of his first novel. Presently he was dancing circles around the aged Mr. O'Leary and Gus from Queens, the doddering and highly inefficient pair who made up the core of the mail room "force." Finishing his chores betimes, Frank spent quarter hour after quarter hour AWOL from the mail room and in the back reaches of the eighteenth floor.

There, I hung out at the world's least busy reception desk, across the way from Betty Guyer, the fashion department assistant, who also had long lag times between the big shows, spring and fall, and the Christmas shopping column. We played games of B for Botticelli that went on for days. It finally took some devious twists of the truth for Frank to fox me on the composer of "The Star-Spangled Banner." He insisted it was Puccini and brought me a score from *Madama Butterfly* to prove it. Outfoxed!

Frank was fun and I was crazy about him, but puzzled over his clear signaling that ours was to be a brother-sister relationship. I decided he was self-conscious about his height, though he seemed fine with our going out together, me rising ever so slightly over him in my heels. Frank was determined on "wising me up" to the delights of the Big Apple. He said he got a kick out of showing the Iowa girl the bright lights of the city. Our blowout the night before he left for Germany was a doozy. His posting had come through, for West Berlin, over which he was ecstatic. An opera fan, he knew he'd be going to a town crawling with concert halls and three opera companies, not to mention Brecht's Berliner Ensemble.

That evening began with straight-up martinis at the bar of the Charles French Café in the Village, followed by veal piccata at Marta's. Then a taxi up to the old Met and a pair of aisle seats to Maria Callas's second-ever Met *Tosca,* from row B of the orchestra. We wound up the evening—the early morning, actually—with Bobby Short and Mabel Mercer at the Blue Angel.

What an evening! What a hangover!

But Frank did not stop at educating me into culture in New York only. He corresponded faithfully from his new spot in Berlin, heard all about my romance with Evan, insisted on booking my hotel in the Berlin portion of my grand tour and handling all the tickets for our three operas and one recital during my four days there. (The Brecht theater, alas, would be dark on the dates I would be there.)

I last saw Frank Cucci walking on the Brooklyn Promenade one windy day in the March following our Berlin escapade. Catching the merest flick of a glance, which could have been Frank seeing me out of the corner of his eye, I flashed on how I would smile in delight, how he would introduce me to his companion, how the elegant man would bend slightly toward me as if he were going to raise my hand to kiss it or simply brush it lightly with his lips. Frank would ask me to lunch with him the following week . . .

But none of it happened. They were abreast of me for a moment, only yards away, but they walked on, never slowing by a hairbreadth.

The scene persisted in my mind long after it had faded from my vision. Something about the way they had walked together, seeming to share a secret, made me realize the truth. Frank, I saw now, played for the other team, as we put it back then. I lost so many simpatico beaux that way. Made me, on occasion, feel and behave like a sore loser.

After the Promenade incident I was not surprised never to hear from him again.

I'd had a letter of stinging rebuke Frank sent when he heard I'd swallowed my pride and gone back to dating Evan again, even after his deception was exposed. I'd also hinted at the turn I was taking as slut of the year in the wake of it. Is this what all his careful mentoring had come to? he wrote. He was furious, he was let down. He was through.

But most broken relationships have codas, and ours was no exception. In 1983 I nearly jumped out of my chair as I watched the credits of a much-hyped made-for-tv movie called *Svengali.* It was adapted from the du Maurier novel *Trilby* and written, I discovered, by Frank Cucci. Peter O'Toole played Svengali, and his young protégée was played by a plump Jodie Foster, just out of Yale and still recovering from the trauma of John Hinckley Jr. Neither actor was up to form, and the whole enterprise seemed weighted down by a ponderous and pretentious script.

I felt bad for Frank then, and again when I looked him up on the

Web recently and learned that he had two or three other screen and television credits, each effort dominated by big-name stars doing flop turns. His date of death was given as July 1989. He would have been fifty-four years old. Just barely.

Meanwhile, back in 1959, Gotham's newest party girl put lemon in the rinse to lighten the blond in her hair, added a touch of shadow to the lids of vaguely Egyptian-looking mascara-outlined eyes. My long ponytail was looped winsomely over one shoulder, and my earlobes were adorned with gold or silver hoops or chunky clasp earrings of the kind favored by Eve Arden and Joan Crawford in *Mildred Pierce.* My partying mates (whose names have been changed) were a high-caliber assortment—they made, I thought, for a nice variety. There was Maury, the Village Democratic activist, a well-brought-up, ambitious Jewish boy, an Ed Koch with testosterone, who was so proud of his erection that he lit a candle to it and posed it above his upright organ as he marched into my bedroom for more. There was Bob M., an up-and-coming editor at Random House, very popular with other guys and with women, too—he was small and wiry, sort of a Steve McQueen without the cool. We never made it in bed, however, his amorous intent undone by his heavy drinking. The others drank also, but not to the point of incapacitation—which may have been Bob's unconscious design.

There was the friend of my friend Gloria, another Jewish lad—these boys were notably more aggressive lovers than their Gentile counterparts, and good at it, too—whom I shall call Saul, who liked to go out for cream cheese and lox after intercourse. There was the best-looking Ivy Leaguer in my stable, a Jack Kennedy look-alike from the architecture school at Yale who took me to a party in

Princeton. All momentum, either for our tryst or for the party, was spoiled by an endless train ride. In a hot railcar that spent a great deal of time on a siding, my date began to assess all the ways in which my costume, haircut, makeup, and midwestern manners fell short of the Ivy League hottie he would have liked to be bringing to the party. It was, once we got there, not a success. Nor, when we got back to my apartment late that night, was it the long-lasting romp usual to the men of my acquaintance or—why deny it—to me?

In late February I went to a party in the staff lounge at one of the large hospitals in the city, given to celebrate the engagement of a male intern to a female resident. There I met an Anglo-Italian doctor. Marco, handsome and otherwise extremely fit, had lost one leg below the knee. He had been a paratrooper, and his plane was shot down on the eastern front as he prepared to make a routine jump, the final one of hundreds he'd made in World War II. I got drunk, and we wound up in bed in one of the private patient suites. Marco was not connected any longer to the New York hospital whose hospitality we were enjoying, his career having taken him, some months before, to a position as staff surgeon at a hospital in another Middle Atlantic state.

He came up to New York for our dates on a weekly basis. In a sublime act of insouciance he would unstrap his prosthesis and hop into bed, where the loss of his lower limb impeded his lovemaking not a whit. Marco was frank about his hedonism, as about everything else. Uncircumcised, and proud of it—he thought the intact foreskin intensified his pleasure—he never used a condom, said it was like making love through a sock. He convinced me that it was not necessary to practice contraception, since as a physician he was well enough versed in the physical signs of ovulation not to impregnate me.

We dined out a good deal and, after the first two weekends or so, took to choosing ever larger and noisier restaurants as it became convenient to let other people hold the conversation for us. Our own conversation had disappointed each of us in different ways. I complained that he told me too many times how he had interned in Paris and fixed up Errol Flynn so he could go on swashbuckling his way through Europe and Hollywood without incurring further paternity suits. He said I told him too many times how much I liked reading Henry James. We got on together not at all well. One cold night in March, after a weekend in a hotel, spent chiefly quarreling over why we were there, he discovered I had missed a period, examined me briefly, and determined that I was indeed pregnant. Not to worry. He was a physician, wasn't he?

After that, he went away for a spell and wrote me a long letter confessing that he could not make "an honest woman" of me because he was already married. His letter explained that in fact his knocked-up wife's posse of brothers had all but waved shotguns in his face to ensure that he made one of *her.* I did not doubt it had been her advanced stage of pregnancy that had quickened his interest in our rendezvousing in New York. Now that this avenue of release was becoming complicated, he refused to become either contrite or falsely seductive. He wrote that he was prepared to administer a perfectly safe medication that would induce a miscarriage and that he intended to do so the next time he could get a weekend off.

Several more weeks went by. A letter from Marco announced that his wife had delivered a healthy baby, a daughter. Late in the first week of the next month, a "medical emergency" presented him the opportunity for a trip to New York, and on May 6 he arrived and the medication was administered. Upon his advising me to seek diversion while it "worked," we went to see *The Man with the Green Carnation,* the Oscar Wilde movie with Peter Finch, then playing at the Plaza. I got home just in time to hemorrhage. Marco offered to come back up if there were complications, but there were none.

Soon, there was Barry, the (to me) really attractive type of older man, gray at the temples, in well-cut tweeds. Barry got more of an ego boost than he should have from his famous dad. His father, a Broadway lyricist, had once written a hit song with Yip Harburg. Barry took me to the theater and dinner at El Morocco, which was handy because his rather elegantly furnished bachelor pad with the mirror over the fireplace was just upstairs. He had shared it until earlier that year with his now ex-wife, a TV anchorwoman. A man in mourning really, Barry was sterile, though far from impotent. His unreachable sadness over this was a revelation to me: it turned out that men, as well as most women, yearned for offspring. Myself, that spring, not so much.

That was about it for lovers between Evan's two-timing me and my next long-term beau Fritz's coming along. Oh, no, I am forgetting my *New Yorker* pal "Seth," who took me to a New Year's Eve party given by A. J. Liebling and Jean Stafford. Afterward, Seth fed me enough coffee at his place to make it OK in his gentlemanly opinion for us to go to bed. My headache the next morning was monumental. I got home just in time in the late afternoon to be reminded by the doorbell of a date with Barry, who came in for some hair of the dog and of course some time in the sack.

It was this disheartening period of my life and these characters that I depicted—though without a trace of understanding or compassion for anyone involved—in that discarded novel. Professor Blum had it right: why would I ask any reader to waste time with them?

The good thing about this period of acting out, this radical excursion outside my own comfort zone, was that it precipitated a crisis of faith. I had fallen away from the Sunday-school brand of Lutheranism that I had practiced when living at home and on weekend visits back there. I skipped religious observances while at the university, where, frankly, it was very unhip to attend church or, John Berryman's classes excepted, to take seriously the presence in the universe of a Creator or of the individual moral conscience. I arrived in New York completely rudderless. That moment to which Saint John of the Cross was referring when he spoke of "the dark night of the soul" never comes to most of us, not because we experience no comparable state, but because we find it hard to justify the grandeur of the phrase. Philosophers, men of genius, and kings may despair; the rest of us usually just give up hope. For me that moment came one Thursday night or, rather, early one Friday morning in the late spring of my twenty-second year. It came to the crude accompaniment of a scratchy show tune on the phonograph, the crude and automatic motions of a man called Johnny moving mechanically above me. I could not recall how Johnny had come to be there. This frightened and appalled me. Frank Cucci's attempts at sophisticating me notwithstanding, I found out, in my long-deferred examination of conscience, that I was not cool and never would be, at least not in the sense of blasé.

My "dark night" ushered in a long weekend of self-examination and a visit, the following Sunday, to the Fifty-Fourth and Lexington Lutheran church, the one handiest to the E train (in at Fourteenth Street, out at Lex and Fifty-Third). This in turn resulted in a first stirring of renewed attention to my baptismal/confirmation vows and a rededication to the tenets of the Nicene Creed. As in the case of C. S. Lewis, the promptings of my soul were not Pauline—not accompanied by lightning bolts on the road to Damascus; rather, as Lewis puts it, the change from the darkness of unbelief into "the light of reality" was more like the transition from the unreal world of dreams to the state when, "after a long sleep, still lying motionless in bed," I became aware that I was now awake. This did not mean I knew who, exactly, that "I" was, but I had a grip on my actions and a renewed sense of responsibility for them. Whoever this person I walked around in was, I was not, after that annus horribilis of 1959–60, any longer prone to destroy her.

Back on Reception

In 1959 *The New Yorker* obtained premises formerly leased by Exide Battery and turned the area into offices for its growing editorial staff. I returned to my job on the now expanded eighteenth floor as to a haven. Life in the fast lane, I decided, was not for me. A girl could get hurt out there.

One day, shortly after the job switch was made, Joe Anthony (Sheila McGrath's predecessor as office manager) brought around a bright pink card that would allow my employer to deduct one dollar a week from my salary toward a retirement fund for me.

"Take my advice," he said kindly. "You need every penny of your salary now, and you are never in this world going to stay here long enough to need a pension." Thanks, Joe. Yet really, who could have predicted the cost of that unsigned card?

My stint in the art department did produce one positive result. While I worked there, I was treated by others on the staff as an equal, and the pattern of acceptance was never quite reversed by my return to the rank of receptionist. This often redounded to my benefit. Perks came my way in the form of invitations to share the opera seats and intermissions in the green room with the music critic, good tables and entrées to discos with the nightclub critic, tickets to art openings and movie screenings, and caviar and perfume from the fashion department goody bags at Christmastime, not to mention the favorable aura that seemed to settle like a mantle over me the moment my turn came in social introductions to say where I worked.

Frank Modell, with whom Evan and I had occasionally double-dated when together, continued to treat me as a friend. Realizing, perhaps, that I had been given a raw deal by Evan, Frank was generous and sweet as well as very funny on the subject. He and I established ourselves in the more staid offices of the nineteenth floor (Mr. Shawn's floor) as "rowdies" when, in December, at the instigation of Brendan Gill, the two of us began organizing a Christmas party. It was to take place in the hall outside the mail room, using the counter in front of the newspaper files as a bar. Jack Kahn's schoolboy sons, on a vacation visit to their pa, volunteered to help decorate with the crepe paper bells and strings of holly-entwined lights I'd provided from a lunch-hour trip to the five-and-dime.

Frank drew wonderful cartoon invites for the three editorial-floor bulletin boards. A buxom female form stood opposite a male form in a suit, both of them cut off above the neck, toasting each other with glasses held at clinking level—the hour and place and date of the festivities inked in below. It was the posting of the one on nineteen that got us into trouble with Mr. Shawn. Lou Forster, his aide-de-camp, came down the back stairs to deliver the kibosh.

"Miss Groth?" he queried, and when I copped to being she, he informed me that Mr. Shawn had "decided that we just can't have this kind of office party here at *The New Yorker.* It would put the publication in too embarrassing a position if we were to be discovered throwing the very sort of office Christmas party the magazine has always satirized in its cartoons."

I couldn't believe my ears, but soon Brendan came shuffling down the staircase to weigh in with a sardonic wag of his head: "It's true, I'm afraid. The whole thing is off."

Jack's sons were devastated. I felt pretty low, too, as I took down the last of the streamers and threw them in the trash. A few rebellious souls stood around at about five o'clock, drinking a little smuggled-in whiskey out of paper cups, but the point had been made and carried. I still have one of Frank's posters, though.

At first I feared that the more lasting result of the episode was to be the impression Mr. Shawn retained of me as a wild cannon on eighteen. But as the months and years went by, and word floated up to him (as he always found ways for it to do), he began to manifest more confidence in my discretion. When one of the staff writers' wives suspected her husband of cheating on her and he hadn't come home to dinner by 10:30 p.m., she called Mr. Shawn, and Mr. Shawn called me. I did what I could to suggest that the wife in question was overreacting. He called me again when Frank Modell was not answering his phone on the morning of a day when he was expected to attend the art meeting. I was elected to go down to his apartment, where I found a tousled Frank, sheepishly discovering that his receiver had been knocked off the hook and he had failed to notice. He was just sleeping in.

A more attractive aspect of my job came in the form of invitations to book parties. I think it may have been in October 1962, when St. Clair McKelway's *The Edinburgh Caper* was being published in book form, that "Mac," as his friends called him, threw a big cocktail party in his suite at the Hotel Adams and invited me.

The Hotel Adams is no more, but in the sixties it was still a mostly residential hotel on the Upper East Side, a slightly less expensive alternative to the Stanhope. Even so, it was not cheap, and I wondered if this grandly catered affair accounted for the spectacular tab he ran up on his drawing account at the magazine. I knew of the McKelway penchant to live beyond his means when in the manic phase of his bipolar disorder. But since he wrote *The Edinburgh Caper* under the delusion that he was part of an international conspiracy, I suppose it came under the heading of professional expenses.

Mac was a handsome, well-dressed chap who sported Scottish forebears and seemed entirely plausible in the role of inactive military officer, which he was. While he was vacationing in Edinburgh during the last year of the Eisenhower presidency, his active imagination got to work cooking up a dandy conspiracy. ("Active imagination" was the euphemism he used to describe his periods of delusional grandeur; today we would say he was "off his meds.") *The Edinburgh Caper* involved a plan to kidnap, perhaps even assassinate, President Eisenhower, the Queen of England, and the Duke of Edinburgh. That McKelway and *New Yorker* readers should derive pleasure from a plot to assassinate a US president underscores the happily ignorant state Americans then enjoyed. The next year that would change.

Mac's brow was unclouded that October evening. He seemed serenely untroubled by the cost as he greeted the thirty or so guests standing around in his large chintz living room. Many notables in publishing were there, among them a number of the writers from the eighteenth floor: E. J. Kahn Jr. and his first wife, Ginny; Berton Roueché and his wife, Kay; Robert Coates; and two or three others, including a tall, ruddy-faced young Talk reporter named (after his maternal grandfather) Grover Cleveland Amen. Grover would later see me home in a taxi, very properly walking me to my door and leaving me at it. Robert Lescher, then an editor at Holt and later to head his own literary agency, was there with Mary Cantwell. They were to divorce some years later, and she would write a vivid account of their marriage, their bookish Greenwich Village world, and their breakup in her *Manhattan Memoir.*

White-jacketed waiters circulated expertly around the crowded room, offering trays of canapés on toast points and Ritz crackers. (In that era, Ritz had pretty much cornered the snack cracker market, now so overabundant with herbal and spiced variations.) Drinks, passed on separate trays, consisted of a heady array of daiquiris, martinis, manhattans, and Tom Collinses. Almost no one seemed to be drinking anything soft, and there was no wine on offer. This was a crowd that had learned to drink in the twenties and, with drying-out respites from time to time, was hard at it still. All this was accompanied by the enthusiastic smoking of cigarettes, people somehow managing to juggle everything yet seldom spilling their drinks. The room became, naturally, increasingly smoky, as well as noisy and laughter-filled. By 8:15 p.m. the crowd was just beginning to thin, the waiters circling mostly to collect glasses and napkins. Able, for the first time, to see over to the other side of the room, I noticed a buzzing cluster of people paying rapt attention to a tiny, watery-eyed woman dressed in black, sitting on a sofa with a gray poodle by her side. This could only be Dorothy Parker, of the wickedly funny bons mots. The only Parker mot I could summon up was "Men don't make passes at girls who wear glasses." Since I was still three or four years away from the day when a combination of myopia and astigmatism would force the dreaded glasses on my nose, I recited this to myself with equanimity. I felt a shiver of excitement as I realized there was an empty seat on that very sofa, just on the poodle's right. After standing on high heels for two hours, I overcame my shyness and took it.

I remember mumbling something complimentary to Mrs. Parker (as everyone called her) and getting a bleary nod in return. Talk swirled around us, and Mrs. Parker's head—rather small and tightly permed—dropped forward onto the white lace collar of her dark dress. I thought perhaps she was asleep. Somebody introduced the smudge-colored poodle to me as Cliché. The poodle remained impassive. Noting a box of dog biscuits open on the coffee table, I took one and, holding it out, asked, "Want a biscuit, Cliché?"

Quick as a flash, Mrs. Parker's head came up, her eyes now glittering icily through what seemed permanent tears. She barked in a voice I was sure was heard all over the room, "It's not a biscuit, for Christ's sake. It's a bickie! Who d'you think you are, Henry James?" Blood rushed to my face as I hastened to correct myself and offer the dog its rightly named morsel. Thank the gods, Cliché took it and the moment passed. I realized, even then, that I had been granted a sort of dubious distinction: I had been put down by the queen of the game.

I loved my little outpost down on the writers' floor and the sense it gave me of being in the center of things. When J. D. Salinger needed to find the office Coke machine (there wasn't one), I was the girl he asked. When Woody Allen got off the elevator on the wrong floor—about every other time—I was the girl who steered him up two floors where he needed to be. When Don Stewart was dating Jean Seberg and she needed to use the ladies' room, I was the girl who unlocked it for her. When Maeve Brennan was homeless and sleeping on the couch in Jack Kahn's office, she, too, found her way to the ladies' john with a key from me. When Leonard Bernstein wanted to make sure his kid brother, Burt, knew he loved him, Lenny called me. When James Thurber needed emergency office space, I was the one who knew that Robert Coates was away and slipped him into Coates's office so he could put one of his last pieces for the magazine—"The Watchers of the Night"—to bed. When Delmore Schwartz was found dead in his hotel room, I was the one who located Dwight Macdonald to go over and pick up the pieces.

A natural progression from such perfunctory but personal contact sometimes led to more substantial involvement in the writers' work. This might, and in fact did, take the form of producing pasteups for Whitney Balliett's books on jazz, suggesting chapter arrangement for Emily Hahn's *Look Who's Talking!*, finding a German translator for Jack Kahn's use in his profile of Arthur Loeb Mayer, running a small lending library of classics and *New Yorker* authors. And sometimes it led to involvement in the personal lives of those I served and theirs in mine.

When I couldn't get an answer from Columbia to my request for an application to their grad school, Dwight Macdonald wrote a scorching letter to his pal Jacques Barzun, likening me to Joseph K. and Columbia to a dark bastion of byzantine bureaucracy. From the day I chided him on making political criticism his forte and yet refusing to do his duty as a citizen and vote, Dwight was always deferential to me in an amused way. He consulted me for suggestions for his book of literary spoofs, an anthology for Random House called *Parodies,* and even used some of them: Chaucer's tale of Sir Thopas and excerpts from Jane Austen's *Northanger Abbey*. He inscribed the British edition of *Against the American Grain* to me as "the Egeria" of the eighteenth floor. I had to look her up in a classical dictionary, but I didn't tell him that. Turns out she was counselor to a king.

When Dwight was reviewing movies for *Esquire,* he continued to write pieces for Mr. Shawn and used the same office while wearing both hats. In the late 1960s *The New Yorker* supported a virtual cottage industry of movie reviewers right there on eighteen. Pauline Kael and Penelope Gilliatt, who split the magazine's reviewing chores, also had offices there, so quite a number of movie people as well as writers like Michael Crichton came through. Burt Lancaster, stung by something Dwight had written about his performance in *The Train,* paid him a visit and, Dwight said later, "tried earnestly to change my mind."

As for Miss Gilliatt and Miss Kael, they couldn't have been less alike. I was not the only one around the office who feared conflict if their paths should cross. Both were tiny women, and both had a species of red hair; but physical size and coloring aside, the two women were like chalk and cheese, in their personalities, their writing styles, and their responses to films. Miss Gilliatt reeked of class (quite literally, as she moved in a cloud of expensive perfume), while Miss Kael was feisty West Coast blue collar all the way. Their differences made for an interesting contrast in the magazine's film coverage. It also led to interesting complexities when one of them was in the position of reviewing movies intimately associated with the other.

When Miss Gilliatt was living with Mike Nichols, he was directing *Catch-22,* and the review fell during Miss Gilliatt's six-month stint. Susan Lardner was asked to review it, presumably to avoid any conflict of interest yet keep the Gilliatt-Kael boundaries in place. Miss Gilliatt later lived with the *New York Times* movie critic Vincent Canby. It was widely believed that Mr. Canby was gay, so when Miss Gilliatt wrote the screenplay for the film *Sunday, Bloody Sunday,* a delicate web of crosscurrents accompanied Miss Kael's review into print. The movie was about the plight of a woman who bonds with her boyfriend's gay lover when he jilts them both. Miss Kael wrote that seeing the film was "like reading a novel that was very far from my life and my temperament," which might have boded an unfriendly response. Yet she found that it cohered, and wrote, "Yes, there's something there, there's truth in it."

Miss Kael worked briefly as a consultant to Warren Beatty. When Beatty's film *Reds* opened in 1981, it may well have been Miss Gilliatt's job to review it. However, she had been removed from the job by that time, the consequence of an unfortunate similarity between some paragraphs of her Graham Greene profile and one that had appeared in *The Nation* a couple of months before. So Miss Kael reviewed *Reds* herself, conflict of interest be damned, and Miss Gilliatt stuck to fiction, at Mr. Shawn's request. Yes, a dicey situation all around, and I couldn't figure out how they worked it so as never to be in the ladies' room at the same time.

I deemed it part of my job to "make nice" with everyone. Miss Kael and I had a jolly time sharing a table and some stiff manhattans at her first anniversary party. When Penelope's nanny Christine had dental appointments and couldn't look after Penelope's six-going-on-seven-year-old daughter, Nolan—her daughter with the playwright of *Look Back in Anger,* John Osborne—Nolie sat at my desk and spent many an afternoon with me. She was very independent and didn't require much in the way of attention, but I suppose it was those afternoons that led to my attending her seventh birthday party. It was held in the spacious digs Penelope had at that time on Central Park West. The adults present sipped Black Velvets (a combination of Guinness and champagne), and they were a starry bunch—Maggie Smith, Betty Comden, and Adolph Green, among others. Woody Allen sat with the children on the floor in front of the screen when we all watched a thirty-three-millimeter cut of *Young Frankenstein*. Long before the days of the flat-screen or the DVD.

But Nolan Osborne was only one of a number of eighteenth-floor offspring in whose lives I played a part. Perhaps it was the distance in miles from my own family that led to my closeness with the children of my "charges" at *The New Yorker*. Alice Trillin thought it would be good for her daughters, Sarah and Abigail, to experience some of the domestic rites surrounding Christmas among Christians, so she arranged to bring them up to my apartment (I was living on Eighty-Fifth Street in Yorkville at the time) to roll out, decorate, and bake ginger cookies with me. We used my grandma's recipe and put on white icing and red-and-green sprinkles. Sarah did the trees, Abigail the Santas, and I finished up with the stars. We did the same thing the next Easter with eggs and dye, using wax crayons to print our names on the eggs we decorated. I knew, to a greater or lesser extent, the children of a number of eighteenth-floor writers: Dwight's sons, Nicholas and Michael Macdonald; Richard Rovere's daughter, Ann; and of course my pals the Kahn boys. I also knew Bernard Taper's sons, Mark and Philip, quite well and went up to the Rudolf Steiner School to watch them in a puppet show they wrote, costumed, and directed.

One of the things I appreciated most about the receptionist job was the way it expanded to allow me to try on a half dozen or so alternate lives. There is something special about the responsibilities that rest with a house sitter, I discovered. No one, not the best friends of the writers involved, not even the nosy dinner guest taking an illicit peek into the medicine cabinet, ever gets a more inside view of the writers' lives than the person given their keys while they are away. Certainly whenever I was that person my house-sitting duties became a sacred trust. In return, I felt that, along with the new closeness I felt to the owners, it gave me a privilege few people ever have—to slip into the artifacts of another kind of life and try it on for size.

Thanks to Tony and Margot Bailey, I know what it is like to live in a historic landmark on the corner of Royal Hill in London's Greenwich postal zone SE10, only a stone's throw from the Greenwich Pier, where the *Cutty Sark* was on display in dry dock and where the Royal Naval Hospital and the Royal Observatory flank the bottom and top of a majestic sweep of lovely English lawn. In the Bailey home I was getting a peep into a gracious living style from Georgian times, translated into a cozier, domestic scale. I loved the peach-colored two-story entrance hall and the little studio off to one side, where Margot kept her paints, her huge potted moose plant, a good few of her paintings, and her favorite P. G. Wodehouse Penguins. I loved taking the Bailey springer spaniel, Daisy, out for her exercise twice a day in Greenwich Park, loved watching Daisy's ears sail out perpendicular to her brown-and-white body as she topped the park's green benches and bounded over beds of roses and impatiens, rushing to answer my call and to snuffle up the dog biscuit (*pace* Mrs. Parker) that was her treat for being such a good girl. The Bailey cat, a neutered ginger male, was suitably imperious and aloof, and the final member of the menagerie, Rocket, was a tortoise with its name in white on its venerable back. Rocket lived under the rhododendron in the back garden and came out for cucumber, lettuce, and other greens daily around five.

The Bailey kitchen was a delight, too, one wall bearing a large amber reproduction of the Bayeux Tapestry, and the opposite wall, open cupboards full of blue-and-white export china, with the wall above the windows a bright, definite red. Upstairs in the large, light master bedroom, I admired the little Rembrandt sketch in brown pen and ink. (Tony began his interest in artist biographies writing pieces about Rembrandt for *The New Yorker* and turned them into two books. He went on to write about other artists, finally producing books on Vermeer, Turner, and Constable, with Velázquez soon to come.)

An exploration of the Bailey linen cupboard, which occupied a prominent large-doored spot opposite the upstairs bath, was an education in itself in how much work it must be to run a household with a husband and three daughters. Noting the occasional darned spot in the all-white towels, I admired Margot's Yorkshire frugality as she kept the same ones going year after year. She chose good quality to begin with, rough cotton terry, scratchy but pure. No noncotton threads need apply.

It was nice, going around Greenwich, from the shops on the high street, to the greengrocer, to the bakery across the road, until the clerks knew me to speak to and pass the time of day. Nice, too, to frequent the neighboring pub for the occasional cheese-and-pickle sandwich in the garden in the rear. It was almost like living an English life of the kind so well drawn in the Christie, Marsh, and Sayers mysteries I often went to sleep with. By the same token, the six weeks I'd spent living in rooms at Exeter College, Oxford, dining in Hall, and having coffee in the Common Room had given me a glimpse of English university life. I owed that glimpse not to a house-sit but to a course I took in English linguistic history the summer of 1966—the summer of the county ball.

My Italian adventure came the year I spent from November through April in Cortona, Tuscany. I was house-sitting a restored fifteenth-century farmhouse for the writer Ann Cornelisen, a wonderful gig I was put on to by my Talk of the Town chum Jane Boutwell. Built of local stone, it nestled up against the tower of a grand edifice known simply as the Palazzone. My Christmas cards that year had the best return address ever, and I loved feeling my way into the life, modern and medieval, still to be sensed among the stones of the interior stairway, the walk-in fireplace, and the giant white porcelain bathtub. Hand-painted crockery, homegrown wine and olive oil, free-range eggs and chickens were all laid on. I luxuriated in having the house cleaned and my clothes and cooking done for me by a *contadina* of leathery skin and a near-toothless but beaming smile. Those Cortona days were magic. I was sorry I couldn't share them with every one of the people I loved.

In New York, while still going to the office daily, I several times moved my stuff to Calvin and Alice Trillin's house on Grove Street to keep it safely lived in while the family was away. At work, Bud's office was messy, even to the point of decrepitude. Bud (as Calvin Trillin was known around the office) covered an old studio couch in brown corduroy and then covered that in hundreds of regional and community newspapers he collected as he gathered stories for his Letters from America series. But at home, where Alice (whom he called "the conscience of Grove Street") was also the decorator, all was a symphony of tasteful, unpretentious comfort with American colonial touches. There I found that Alice and the girls were in evidence all around me just as they appeared in Bud's references to them in his food pieces, later gathered in books like *Alice, Let's Eat* and *American Fried.* I'd been to the *American Fried* book party held in the Central Park Zoo, and there were amazing things to eat, all deep fried and spread out on checkered tablecloths within roaring distance of the zoo cats. Back on Grove Street, the Trillin freezer held a full cache of wondrous bagels, which meant I didn't have to go out on Sunday mornings in the rain.

Jane Kramer has written about fabulous Thanksgiving dinners she has served in distant places around the world and in her West Side digs in Manhattan. I know the New York digs firsthand from a summer when I house-sat and dog-sat for the family dog. Romeo was a large Normandy sheepdog called a Bouvier des Flandres, who spoke only French. My own French improved that summer, at least in the imperative mode. As I worked on "Assieds-toi, Romeo!" (sit), "Romeo, arrête!" (stay), and "Viens ici, Romeo!" (come here), I got acquainted with a New York subculture of dog walkers on the dog runs of the park.

Much later, Jane's fond recall of the idiosyncrasies of her two-oven stove—frequently on the blink—brought back memories of my own timid tryouts of some simple summer meals in the best-equipped kitchen I'd ever seen. Think Julia Child plus Mario Batali. Jane was living part of the year in Paris, and accustomed to French cuisine, she'd brought back duplicates of every piece of equipment she'd need for those dishes in America, then did the same with the pots and utensils from the summer house in Todi. All that, and my needs seldom stretched beyond a pot for pasta and a pair of salad tongs.

Back on eighteen, the coffee and tea and cocoa on offer at a hot plate in the hall was run by me not as a concession but as my home kitchen. I spent hours one Christmas agonizing over which coffee mugs I could afford to buy to present to my favorites, five denizens of the floor—all men. There was the senior editor William Knapp; the staff writers Bernard Taper, Jack Kahn, and Kevin Wallace; and the art department's caption editor, the comic novelist Peter De Vries.

Bill Knapp, a great wearer of suits, had the look of one of those bankers who Jack had suggested in his memoir could reasonably be expected to turn in at the yacht club on West Forty-Fourth. He probably should have worked out more, and his high color was not a sign of ruddy good health. I think it was those hours he spent giving sensitive editorial strokes to Bob Shaplen's Letters from Southeast Asia. The copy came in close to deadline; again and again, Bill missed his train to Greens Farms Road in Westport to stay and get it ready for print. I let him buy me a lunch or a drink from time to time because I knew it gave him pleasure to flirt with me in an uptight WASP way and I was too weak to deny him, and myself, that boost.

Bernard Taper, whose profile subjects included Balanchine and

Pablo Casals, flirted more outrageously—he was, after all, a handsome fellow, the son of a well-connected California family, and his Jewish mother, like many a Jewish mother before her, had raised her son to believe he was a king. A nice king, but with royal prerogatives. I was not so inclined to accept those invitations because Tape, as we called him, had a wife named Phyllis who was my chum. As the not-as-handsome spouse—her best feature was a glowing smile—Phyllis seemed both brainy and vulnerable, and I sensed that Tape was the center of her emotional life. That may have been true of Peggy Knapp up in Westport as well, but she was a whiskey-voiced woman with plenty of confident swagger and I didn't feel as protective of her.

Jack Kahn was one of the few people in the office who called Mr. Shawn "Bill." They went way back together, to the days when Shawn edited Jack's dispatches from Europe during World War II.

After Harold Ross died and Shawn became editor in chief, a formality descended over his editorship that made it extremely difficult for even six-footers like Bob Shaplen to be anything but deferential in their dealings with him. Jack knew it pissed off his mates down on eighteen when he stopped in their doorways to announce casually that he was on his way up to nineteen to "see Bill." So he did it every time. This gave him a gleeful kind of boyish pleasure, but I think it also cost him. Some resentment came his way because of it, and his reputation took some rather cruel and easy hits when he sold a three-part piece on Coca-Cola, and then went on to sell three-parters on corn, wheat, and ultimately the foodstuffs of the world. The other boys were not amused.

But then, as a short and feisty bantamweight, Jack had fought his way out of rougher playgrounds than theirs, and he had the last laugh. Over the course of his fifty-six years at the magazine, he saw many more of his own pieces get into print than did anyone else—amounting to three million words, all told. He also published a number of books, including not one but two on his favorite subject: *About the New Yorker and Me: A Sentimental Journey* (1979) and *Year of Change: More About the New Yorker and Me* (1988).

Five feet five, trim and tanned, with crinkly, sandy hair and crinkly eyes—the eyes were blue with amber lights—Jack was both a man's man and a great favorite with women as well. The son of the well-known New York architect Ely Jacques Kahn, Jack was as close to being a charter member of the New York Jewish elite (written about in Stephen Birmingham's *Our Crowd*), as you get, but had less side than anybody on the floor. Feisty, yes; snooty, no.

I liked Jack a lot and got along well with both Ginny and Ellie, as his second wife Eleanor was called. It was Ellie who saw to it that I was invited to their big annual cocktail party and even bigger New Year's Eve parties. These were laid-back but amply catered affairs where one might gaze around the room and see the likes of Teddy White, Walter Cronkite, a Broadway actress or two, and of course Jack's illustrious sisters, the painter Olivia Kahn and Joan Kahn, who had her own mystery imprint at Harper.

When Jack learned that I would be leaving the magazine to take an assistant professorship at the University of Cincinnati, he went to considerable lengths to "launch" me in Cincinnati society. I was an overnight guest of his and Ellie's at the Kahn place in Truro. Jack baked one of his famous clam pies—or six of them, more like—hosting a large group of regular summer residents on the Cape who hailed from Cincinnati, people who served on the symphony board and represented the A-list of the Cincinnati social scene, all of whom had me round for dinner when I got out to my new home. It was a typically warm gesture from a warm and lovely man.

I was shocked and sad to read of Jack's death in 1994 at the age of 77. A bad auto accident, and Ellie had to bear not only his loss but the burden of having been behind the wheel. Ellie is a strong woman, however, and she has borne up bravely in the sometimes difficult role of survivor. She gets finely and fiercely angry when she feels Jack has been underappreciated at the magazine.

Peter De Vries, the author of *Comfort Me with Apples* and half a dozen other terrific comic novels, was a man of fine instincts. Never willing to fob off gift giving to a salesperson, he always asked for "tips" and, when told I liked Elizabeth Bowen, got me a book by Elizabeth Bowen or, following other tips, an album of lieder or some Monteverdi on Deutsche Grammophon. His and his wife's agonizing loss of their daughter to leukemia is rendered beautiful in *The Blood of the Lamb,* and I even liked it in the uneven but wrenching, tragicomic movie with Walter Matthau and Carol Burnett called *Pete 'n Tillie.* His other daughter, Jan, often sat at my desk and chatted with me while waiting for her dad. A son, Jon, is a good actor who has worked with La MaMa and, aptly enough, in Greek tragedy.

Kevin Wallace, another Californian (he'd been brought onboard by his pal Bernard Taper) wrote a lot of fact pieces for the magazine but very seldom appeared in it. Tall and tawny and well connected in California—like Taper, but on the WASP side—Kevin was totally correct yet flatteringly attentive. He was one of the casualties of Mr. Shawn's sadomasochistic streak. Shawn, unwilling to confront a writer's disappointment, would buy long pieces he had no intention of running, let them molder in the "bank," and allow their authors to twist slowly in the wind. Kevin, battling alcoholism on top of this, managed to stay sober, but I think the strain of it may have cost him his marriage. One winter, to preserve his sanity, he rigged up a photography kit modeled after that used by his idol Ansel Adams. With what I thought great skill, he took pictures of me and anybody else he could talk into it. When we found that both of us were planning to attend the anti–Vietnam War November Moratorium in Washington, he arranged for me to accompany him and his son and daughter—both in their teens—on the ACLU's chartered bus. There, on a day so cold that we could see our breath, he shot roll after roll of us amid hundreds of thousands of peaceniks. Kevin finally moved back to his native San Francisco—a place his family practically started, and a place where he was once a popular feature writer on the *Chronicle.* But before he made that belated decision, we spent an evening at the Knapps' country club, where Kevin patiently taught my nearly danceproof feet (and more willing hips) how to rumba.

I thought of these men as quasi–family members. Their affection for me meant the world to me, I did not know why. I suppose they functioned as the brothers, fathers, and husbands of my dreams, and so my Christmas gifts for these five were terribly important. But even I knew it should not matter so much to me that my choice of mugs proved a bad mistake: It was clear I should have gone in for blue, gray, or brown pottery, not the bright ceramic cups on pedestals that screamed California, and Southern California at that. Economy and a momentary lapse of judgment accounted for it, but I suffered greatly as I saw the pained expressions that flitted across the faces of my pets and were as quickly squelched in order to spare my feelings. Nobly, to a man, they stepped up and filled their ghastly vessels of buttercup yellow, persimmon red, pea green, and peacock blue. Men behaving badly? *Au contraire.*

Fritz

I ACQUIRED MY NEXT SERIOUS boyfriend indirectly by way of a Talk reporter named Bill Murray. In those days, men who came up to meet *New Yorker* writers for lunch and arrived early often passed the time chatting with me on my post at the reception desk. Sometimes they even convinced me to go out with them. Murray's too timely friend Cranston, as I shall call him, wanted to put the world back to rights by proving once and for all that Heisenberg's uncertainty principle—the source of all that was wrong with the twentieth century—was mathematically incorrect. He was going to do this despite his lack of academic credentials in the field—hadn't Newton or somebody been without them as well? The pampered son of old-money parents, Cranston may have been certifiable. He was, for sure, bipolar, though he was charming and reasonable enough, when not on his Heisenberg hobbyhorse, and probably had, as he casually informed me, a liberal arts degree from Princeton. He had the tweedy good looks of the Ivy League, to which I had already proved receptive. What's more, he was a man who didn't mind a late lunch with a fellow who didn't mind a late lunch either. When Murray called to say he had been detained on a story and would have to cancel, Cranston asked me to eat with him instead. I went and was sufficiently entertained to accept another date.

The following Sunday he took me to brunch at his brother's loft in SoHo. Three documentary-film makers, the Maysles brothers and Donn Pennebaker, and the Village habitué barkeep Bradley Cunningham were there. Along with one or two other men, and various wives and girlfriends, we sat around knocking back Bloody Marys. Strong ones. The Bloody Marys kept coming. The brunch didn't. My Heisenberg beau soon became too drunk to stand and sank deep into the arms of a wing chair.

One of the other men present was Friedrich Steffan-Freude—a.k.a. Fritz. (His name and those of his family and friends have been changed.) He was a struggling playwright and a master cabinetmaker who, when we met, was building Pioneer Forts ("Perfect for Young Dan'l Boones") at FAO Schwarz. Six feet tall, blond, and handsome, he looked like a cross between the German played by Hardy Kruger in *A Bridge Too Far* and the one played by Marlon Brando in *The Young Lions.* He had the advantage over the movie Germans of being anti-Nazi. Of course I didn't know that then, or anything about him, except the part about his looks. I just thought that as he leaned on one elbow against the room divider that served as a bar, Fritz, in white shirtsleeves and chinos, exuded a raffish European charm. When, at two o'clock, I despaired of ever seeing eggs Benedict, I went over to Cranston and said, "I want to go home." Cranston could not be roused from his snoring collapse. I never saw him again, and as far as I know, Bill Murray never did either.

Fritz stepped up to me and made a small bow. I almost think his heels came together, but in his desert boots it was hard to tell. "I will see you home, *ja*? It is too expensive for me, the taxi, but I will be glad to walk with you." It was a distance of at least a mile and a half, but the day was fair, the man was grand, and I found it an offer I couldn't refuse. He was still finding his way around English, so the conversation was stilted. We tried out some of my German and found that it, too, was pretty rudimentary. However, he took my phone number, and that evening he gave me a call.

"Do I speak to Janet?"

I assured him that he did.

"Here is Fritz. Ah, please, can you tell me how to prepare a beef heart?"

"Do you mean—the heart of a *cow*?"

"I believe that is right, *ja*."

"Well, frankly, Fritz, I haven't the faintest idea," How odd, I thought. It would never have occurred to me to eat a beef heart. "I suppose you've already bought it?"

"Oh, *ja,* it lays already in the oven."

"Well, I'm sorry I can't be of any help. I wish you well with it. Let me know how it turns out."

I asked about the outcome when we had dinner later the same week, and received his assurance that the cow's ticker had been "succulent." After the meal, Fritz suggested a walk. At the corner of West Fourth Street and Washington Square we came across a knot of men playing chess, and as though drawn by a magnet, Fritz steered us toward it. A well-established scene of ad hoc chess games, this area of the park had concrete tables with boards etched in their tops, though players often superimposed their own boards. "Many of these players are quite accomplished," Fritz said after watching awhile. I learned that he played chess the way some men play video games or follow the ponies—that is, incessantly. And he was sufficiently good at it to have been ranked the junior master of Mecklenburg, Germany, in his teens.

Because neither of us had any money to spend on entertainment of the ticketed sort, it became a custom for us, after our eaten-in meals, to take long walks, often ending up downtown in Washington Square Park or some other green square dotting the urban environment. There, the paths and benches offered valuable options for city-dwelling couples, parks being one of the few cost-free environments for holding serious conversation. Bed is practically the only alternative. Kitchens, maybe, but almost nobody in New York has more than a Pullman kitchen. As for living rooms, I've always thought authors of plays set in New York make a mistake locating plays there. Practically all the drama takes place offstage. Restaurants, hotel lobbies, are too noisy. But in a park you can sit down in a place where something is growing and you can talk quietly. Grass and trees make talking quietly make sense. Soon we were meeting for coffee at the Peacock Café, going for long walks around the Village, and ending up at the park.

Fritz loved me first. I was five feet seven, had a 36-26-36 figure, and wore my hair in a twelve-inch blond ponytail. What more did a man need to know? So he loved me before he knew me, and when his growing knowledge seemed to change his love, I held it against him. I held off, got to know him first, and only came to love him with our growing intimacy. Each dubious thing I learned only seemed to endear him to me more. He brushed his hair forward, straight into his face, with mad, compulsive strokes, his face screwed up in an expression of unwavering disgust; he crammed his pockets with screws, nails, money, stamps, envelopes, and string; he was an obsessive pusher-up of the glasses on his nose, grabber of himself about the upper rib cage, flexer of shoulders, scratcher behind the ear, and reader of the last page of every book he picked up.

I see now that I was falling, not only for the idiosyncrasies of a handsome fellow, ten years older than I, but for a European way of life. I had been drawn to it in the books I'd been reading since I discovered Henry James and the Russians in my teens. By linking my life to his, I was trying on a whole new set of identity markers, much more cosmopolitan and sophisticated than any I had acquired as a birthright. It excited and perplexed me in about equal measure.

One evening, Fritz invited me to a party at Brad Cunningham's. It was my one and only pot party. Everybody let me know they thought I was a real prude for not taking my turn at a toke, but judging from the conversation—Pause. "Anybody catch Monk the other night at the Five Spot?" Pause. "Far out, man." Heads nod. Pause—I decided pot was not good for the brain. To me, alcohol was far superior. People improved their talk on scotch and martinis; this was a downer. The apartment was interesting, though, a Village classic of high ceilings, sparse furniture, and large, inscrutable art on the walls. The party was a farewell for Brad and his wife, Jean, who were about to take off for Florida, leaving Fritz in charge. Fritz, I knew, was an accomplished cabinetmaker. He'd quarreled bitterly with his father over his father's participation in Hitler's war effort, and as a result, he wound up with a trade certificate in lieu of a university education. He was going to stay at the Cunninghams' rent-free, house-sitting and doing some cabinetwork. Brad and Jean never did come back and live in that flat, but the island Fritz built—in an eat-in kitchen, no less—undoubtedly upped the selling price when the divorcing couple put it up for sale. I lost track of what became of Jean, but Brad remarried and had a family. His big success came later when he owned and operated Bradley's, a bar on University Place that Nat Hentoff once called "The Perfect Jazz Club."

Among their few furnishings, Brad and Jean had a grand piano, and when I went up to have an after-dinner coffee with Fritz the week following their departure, I discovered that he had made a bed for himself by laying a full-size mattress on the floor under the grand. By now I was quite enamored of the charming Kraut, and we wound up making love under the piano. We had gotten to about the fourth turn in our bolero when I found myself gazing into the eyes of the Cunningham cat, of which Fritz was also in charge. Making love on odd surfaces—or under odd surfaces—became a kind of theme. Down at my place in the Village, where Fritz spent more and more time, it meant making love on top of a door slung over two sawhorses, whose usual function was to serve as a dining table, as well as on a couple of twin couches shoved together, which made up my living room seating. Once, when we both had head colds, Fritz pulled the mattresses off my couches and laid them side by side on the floor, where we tumbled around feverishly between trips to the bathroom, the water jug, and the tissue box. On occasion we even used the bed in my bedroom. It was an odd size, somewhere between twin and full, called a princess. We were a pretty tight fit, which suited us just fine. Between Fritz's pad and mine it was a kind of traveling *Decameron.* We were exciting together sexually, and we made the most of it.

I don't remember when things got more domestic, but we were soon taking all our meals together and all our weekends, too. I found myself clearing my calendar of the remaining unimportant men so

I could be free for Fritz. It may have been my failure to get it absolutely cleared that led to our first quarrel. From one point of view, it was quite dramatic: Fritz threw the Cunningham cat at me. I wasn't hurt, the cat wasn't hurt, but fearing more scratches from an angered feline, I put on my clothes and went home.

In early July, when Fritz's house-sit ended, he came to live with me. He was broke. FAO Schwarz would not start adding new Pioneer Forts to their inventory until October. Fritz and I agreed that he would be the househusband, and he began work on *Peer Gynt,* next up in the series of Ibsen plays he was translating for a German publisher.

One Saturday afternoon he returned to the apartment to hear soft thuds issuing from the kitchen. He stood in the doorway and looked upon a scene of desolation. I was seated cross-legged on the floor, tears rolling down my cheeks, surrounded by fruit, which I was angrily trying to shove into a paper bag.

"Na, what's this?" he asked, sweeping a hand over the narrow kitchen and its contents. "What can be the meaning of this spectacle? Why is honey [as he called me—I called him honey, too] sitting on the floor? Why is she crying? What is she doing with all these fruits?"

"These aren't fruits," I said, choking back tears. "They're *nectarines.* They—they're crosses of peaches and plums. Oh, Fritz, the flavors are just *fighting* with each other in there. Bitter tasting. It's terrible. And the poor pits are grown all out of shape. They must be so confused."

"Are you sure?" asked Fritz.

"I don't have to be sure." I held up a sticky fist and opened it to reveal a large, misshapen stone. "I can see it. And that's not the worst of it. I'm almost sure it can never have little nectarines." More tears.

"Honey," he said, reaching over to extract the pit from my hand and throw it away. "Now, honey, is this not ridiculous to get so sentimental over an inanimate object?"

"It's not inanimate," I objected, sniffing. "It grows."

"Well, just let me help you up here." He steered me to a chair around the corner in the front room. "Now, sit right over here where you won't see them, all right?"

"They could have been just plain peaches or just plain plums. And they'd know what they were. A peach knows how to be a peach. Only those terrible humans come along and mess everything up and try to 'improve' them."

Fritz clapped. "I agree. You are absolutely right on the peach question. Now, please, come out with me, won't you? I will shoot the nectarine man and afterward I will buy you a *granita di caffè* in the Peacock, *nicht*?"

And that is what we did. The coffee ice, not the shooting.

Although Fritz had been in New York only six months at the time of our meeting, he already played an active role in a circle of people who revolved around a couple named Jillian and Hugo Braun. It consisted of emigrated Europeans and of Americans who had done time as expatriates in Europe, many of whom seemed to be the rebellious children of wealthy families in Kansas City. Hugo was built along the lines of Edward G. Robinson, but the other men in the group all had tall, fit bodies going for them, and the women were good at that leotard-wearing, dark-hair-pulled-back-in-a-ponytail look that spelled bohemian chic in the sixties.

Fritz spoke of these people constantly, and Hugo was practically a fixture in our apartment, but my love made no move to introduce me into the larger circle. I would come home to find Fritz and Hugo hunched over the little traveling chess kit Fritz had given me shortly after we met. (My own game had me staving off checkmate OK but never learning to go in for the kill.) Hugo often stayed through dinner and the evening. If he did not stay, Fritz would go to the apartment Hugo shared with Jillian.

True, I had one brief meeting with Jillian and Hugo and one of the former expats named Ruby, which took place in the Braun's apartment. Fritz and I dropped by one evening in the company of the abstract artist we'd dined with, also an expat. But Fritz was mad at the artist, the artist was mad at Ruby, Jillian was mad at Hugo, and Fritz, finding that the rapid-fire exchange of insults outstripped his English, retired into a neutral corner, leaving me in a position that could only be called the lurch.

I felt I'd wandered into a hostile camp, but Fritz later shifted the emphasis to an unfavorable impression *I* had made. How I could have made any impression at all, I was at a loss to explain. However, Fritz said the general agreement on this point had done much to reestablish harmony among the others in subsequent me-less encounters. When I look back on those people now, I don't know why I disliked them so. I believe at bottom there was some leftover feeling of inferiority behind it. They were all, in one way or another, artists or artists manqué. It was clear that I, at twenty-three, was regarded as not having lived enough to be in their league. Unlike Rabe, I had never worked on the waterfront or written a history (unpublished) of the American Civil War in hipsterese. Nor had I lived in Europe for two years like Rabe's ex-wife, Hester, and Hugo, and almost everybody else, except Jillian, who, however, had chalked up three husbands and three divorces, which seemed to balance things out where she was concerned.

Hester was the sister of a famous abstract expressionist. She and Rabe had already decided on divorce when Hester gave birth. Now, meeting in the cozy confines of the Braun circle, they talked happily of how they'd named their daughter the Aztec word for "regret." Hugo, it developed, had once been the lover of Stella, now divorcing Sid. As in all exclusive groups, this one ran to a lot of cross-fertilization. They seemed to like the fact that Fritz had "background" and "breeding," and they thought his rebel stance put him in their own iconoclastic mold. But I thought the whole construct a rationalization on their part. It overlooked the sharp distinction between their minirebellions against their bourgeois families and Fritz's breach with his father. Herr Steffan-Freude was a shipbuilder who switched to aeronautics in the 1920s and became one of the major architects of the bombers that devastated London. The Americans in the Braun circle still enjoyed the fruits of their trust funds, while Fritz, in fact, was disinherited. He was a real rebel. Another reason they liked to have him around was that he was not a proven failure. They read his work. They had the evidence of his sharp perceptions and his original mind. He lent the whole group a welcome air of greatness-to-be.

As to what Fritz saw in them, I grudgingly had to admit that with all the objections one might have to their characters, they made better conversation than most people I knew.

I tried hard, that summer, to reconcile the Fritz I knew when we were alone and Fritz as he behaved when he was the coddled darling of the Braun circle. One evening when I came back to an empty flat from a cocktail party given by a *New Yorker* friend, I started thinking about Fritz's closed circle again. I knew I had made a hit at Ved Mehta's party, and I wanted, more than anything, for Jillian and Hugo Braun to know it, too.

The sensible thing to do, of course, would have been to eat some supper, take a long bath, and go to bed. But I had never been good at the sensible thing, and I now conceived the idea of going over to the Brauns'. People dropped in on them unannounced all the time. Fritz had made a point of extolling this swinging form of informality. So why shouldn't I drop in? These were people who, I had been told, appreciated style. So I would carry it off, with style. Disarm them with gay chatter, amusing anecdotes about James Thurber and E. B. White . . . Perhaps Fritz would be there. It seemed to me he almost always was.

I refreshed my makeup and walked the few blocks to the Brauns'. Even in my slightly elevated condition, I may have lacked the nerve to actually push their doorbell. But as I turned onto their street, I saw Hugo and Jillian crossing from the other side, in my direction, on their way home.

"Why, hello," I said, trying to sound surprised. "I was just thinking of you. As a matter of fact, if I had seen a light on, I would have been tempted to call on you."

They exchanged glances that were too nuanced for me to interpret in my fuzzy state.

"Well," said Jillian, "you're here. We're here. Why not come up with us and have a drink?"

"Delighted," I said, and I followed them into their brownstone.

I had been there for only a quarter hour when Fritz telephoned to say he would drop by. Jillian must have intimated that I was there, for he spoke to me crossly when he walked in the door. *I knew he wouldn't like it,* I thought, *but he doesn't have to show it in front of them.* He brooded over near the fireplace. After a while he announced that he was leaving.

"I'll come with you," I said.

"I don't want you to," he all but snarled.

"Ooh," said Jillian, raising her eyebrows. "Has somebody ever displeased somebody."

"Very well," I said haughtily, "I'll just stay here with these nice people."

Fritz departed. I chattered on. How successfully, I could not tell. It slowly dawned on me that I had openly challenged Fritz's authority. Difficult for an American female to grasp the enormity of that. At the moment, I was only conscious that the impossible had happened. I had committed a social faux pas, and I was uncomfortable over the novelty of it. I had failed myself in many ways, but I had always prided myself on my social acumen, my flair for getting on with diverse types of people. As though if there were a heaven, I might yet get into it by behaving well at teas.

I made my departure, somehow, and went back to my apartment to wait for Fritz. At three o'clock in the morning, he came back home. I'd won. I was no longer excluded from his social life. Almost at once I saw how unimportant it was.

By fall, having sorted out our differing—and now interlocking—circles of friends, we moved to a new, more charming apartment on West Twelfth Street, a block and a half away from the old one. There began a longish happy time of our life together.

Intermezzo

As if to mirror my own happiness that fall of 1960, the world around me seemed to reflect only skies of blue. Beginning with the nomination of John Kennedy, the USA, at any rate, was entering its Camelot period. I hadn't attended the big rally in Herald Square for Jack when he and Jackie campaigned in Manhattan. But I did go to Rockefeller Center on my lunch hour later that afternoon. The presidential candidate was alone and pressing the flesh among a crowd of supporters at the skating rink in front of 30 Rock. I had just a moment in his presence, but that moment brought me into the orbit of a most attractive man who seemed to find me attractive, too. What I had thought of as singling me out, I learned, was more likely the result of meds he took for back pain. Mr. Shawn's then secretary, Pat Broun, who had briefly been employed at the White House, disabused me over lunch one day. She attributed that runaway testosterone—the smile, the intensity—which I'd found so compelling, to prescription drugs. Poor fellow. I would just as happily have gone on in ignorance.

The New Yorker was a solid bastion of blue under Mr. Shawn, who so sympathized with his staff's enthusiasm that he announced (through the switchboard) a time-out for the Inauguration Day ceremony. We all gathered in the checking department (site of the only telly on the premises) to watch John Fitzgerald Kennedy be sworn in. The room was crowded and hot, but totally rapt, we watched the spectacle unfold, and we broke into a spontaneous cheer as the new president said, "Ask not what your country can do for you—ask what *you* can do for your country." There was general satisfaction voiced, too, when he placed a poet in the forefront of national life—at least momentarily—by his nod to Robert Frost.

It may have been about this time that some new faces began to appear around *The New Yorker.* A battery of Talk reporters who had been brought in a few years before I arrived were moving on up to longer pieces or working on their own writing at home. So I missed the days when Anthony Bailey, John Updike, and Jon Swan came in regularly. But Calvin Trillin, John McPhee, and Calvin Tomkins arrived. And Ved Mehta, the sweet-natured, blind, Indian-born chronicler of his own extraordinary life, became a regular on "my" floor in 1961.

Ved never missed a day when he was in the country. His coworkers were not always at their best when coping with Ved. They were jealous of his special, almost father-son relationship with Mr. Shawn and what they considered the inordinate amount of print granted his work. I am sure he knew how many jokes were directed at the visual descriptions (always accurate) in which his writing abounded—his antennae were sensitive enough to permit him to perambulate New York streets without aid. The work itself represents his triumph over all that. We had one emotional dustup out in the corridor in the early seventies. I no longer remember what precipitated it, but I remember vividly our mutual apologies and Ved's weeping and throwing his arms around me and saying, "I love you, Jan." His inclusion of me in the parties he gave, at his first place in the Picasso, and later in the Dakota, always pleased and touched me. I came to know his father and his sister Usha well enough to attend the engagement party Ved threw for Usha and her handsome husband-to-be, a naval officer. Having known them, even a little, has lent an added interest for me to Ved's six volumes of autobiography.

Also among the new arrivals were Henry Cooper, Gerry Jonas, and Bill Wertenbaker—a trio of young writers hired just out of college who were to contribute fact pieces on space, ecology, and water sports, in that order. These fellows were roughly my own age, and I found myself at a number of parties to do with their engagements or weddings and, in one instance, was part of a foursome attending a concert at Carnegie Hall. Nice fellows. I was particularly enchanted to be included in a "sherry party" one Christmas, held in Henry's family's vast apartment on Park Avenue. It must have been there that Henry casually asked if I had plans for the holiday and, learning that I had none, invited me to come by for Christmas "lunch"—a wondrous affair straight out of Dickens (*after* Scrooge sees the light), complete with a golden goose and blazing plum pudding. Three generations of Coopers—whose photos crowded the lid of the closed piano—made me feel welcome and as at home as a girl from Iowa could. Henry was my favorite of the blue bloods I came across—absolutely no side, and he seemed to know I enjoyed the peeks he gave me into his world. Showed me around the family graves on a Saturday trip I once made up to Cooperstown. Yep, James Fenimore and all.

Constance Feeley, too, was one of the new fact writers given an office on eighteen. There were not that many women on the floor and she and I began having the occasional lunch or after-work drink together. As the daughter of a career army officer, Constance had a history as a loner who found it hard to fit in. Once, when she had done a Talk piece on Carlos Montoya, a star of the flamenco guitar, we went to a concert he gave at Carnegie Hall. I discovered a hair trigger to her temper that bordered on the psychotic. She had just such a break with me, flying into a rage when I innocently confused the classical with the flamenco guitar (or perhaps it was the other way around). It was all I, even I, with my vaunted powers as a soother of artistic temperaments, could do to quiet her down and sustain the relationship.

One night she asked me to dinner at her one-bedroom apartment in Murray Hill. I found the whole evening strangely touching. Each doily and cut-glass decanter, each candle on the linen-draped card table with the telltale folding legs and folding chairs, bespoke a hostess unaccustomed to making such efforts. When the bell rang and the lady from the apartment across the hall entered and was introduced to me as Doro Merande, I realized whom the efforts had been made for. Miss Merande was a character actress of great charm and standing, both in Hollywood and on the stage. It was her stories of those places behind the scenes that we had been called together to hear. Doro said she'd suffered great pangs of near sibling rivalry when her sister-under-the-skin—the actress Margaret Hamilton—vied for the same "sour, witchy old women" roles. Margaret, complained Doro, was "not even the prettier of the two of us" but, perhaps just on that account, had won the coveted role of Wicked Witch of the

West in *The Wizard of Oz.* Miss Merande allowed herself the tiniest moment of pique, but that soon gave way to genuine pleasure as we raved about our love for the roles she did win, in *Our Town, The Seven Year Itch,* and *The Man with the Golden Arm.*

We were just finishing up our lemon sorbets when the bell rang again and Constance pressed the buzzer to let up a young man with locks of dirty-blond hair that flopped over sharp features, wearing a white sharkskin suit and holding a white fedora. He was introduced to us as Tom Wolfe, a former colleague of hers at *The Washington Post.* The two had bonded as a couple of gentlefolk braving the rigors of the DC city beat. In a definite Virginia accent, Mr. Wolfe told us he couldn't stay. He was dropping off a manila envelope. I wondered if it was a piece of writing he had asked Constance to get into the hands of the *New Yorker* fact editor. I thought he expressed some bitterness as he turned to leave that, unlike Constance's, his own job application at the magazine had been rebuffed. But I may be mistaken about that.

Fritz: The Denouement

The end of the affair began after Fritz and I had enjoyed three happy years together. Well, two of them were happy. So happy that from my point of view, the natural consequence was marriage. Fritz finished the *Peer Gynt* translation, finished his own play, and began work on some cabinetry in the new apartment. One night, after he and I had been living there for a month or so, I became a full partner in our lovemaking. I just let go and achieved complete surrender. It was as though, all my sexually active life, while experiencing pleasure aplenty, I had had a cramp, and the more I tried to release it the tighter it got, until, not from tiredness, not as a result of default, but from readiness, aware and carefree, I stopped trying and the cramp disappeared.

Fritz was immensely moved. He held my face in his hands and said, "I did not dream that I would one day receive an American girl's first unselfish love."

I beamed.

It was wonderful. It was like discovering the world. More and more I longed to bear him a child, if only I could win his consent. For the first time, I felt confident that I could have a child without turning into the bane of its existence, its mother. As for marrying, with Fritz I saw the possibility of avoiding the lifelong farce of the Happy Home—that conventional kind of marriage entered into for security, merely in order to be safe in a world of manufactured images, where no harm could come to me as I sat in the family bomb shelter, raising my kids on a pack of lies about how swell everything was.

It must have been our third winter when, having been through two holiday cycles of Christmas together and even sent out joint Christmas cards to a select few, I began to make nervous notes in a composition notebook of the kind I still use. Rather pathetic little notes . . .

> Why can't he be sure he loves me? Why can't he make up his mind to marry me? He's like that in everything, of course. He turns and turns things over in his mind till he sees so many possibilities he doesn't know which end is up. I would fall in love with Hamlet. But I am no Ophelia, even though I did damn near send myself down the river over Evan. I would not do it again. He can hang fire all he wants. He can't outlast me. He suspects it, too. He even said to me, "Anyone who cries as easily as you do is pretty tough. You don't give an inch; you give only tears."

One morning I woke from a dream to face Fritz. "Remember that woman we saw last night, sitting at an outside table at the Peacock? The one with the terrific purple cloche that dipped down across one entire half of her face? Well, I dreamed I had one just like it in red. I looked marvelous in it. I was holding our son in my lap—he looked marvelous, too—and you were driving the three of us to New Jersey."

Fritz did not respond. I rose on one elbow and looked at him. "You didn't like that dream, did you?"

"No."

I looked again into the abyss. It was becoming all too familiar. I saw it each time we disagreed or saw things differently and whenever marriage or children were mentioned. Each time I had more to lose. But I also had more to hold on to. I was ready, now, to acknowledge my own strength. I knew that if I had to, I could be alone and remain perpendicular. I was even prepared to reject the idea that if I were to be left alone, I would be unalterably miserable. Kierkegaard had it right. Being is always in a state of tension with nothingness, and the only way over the abyss is a leap of faith. He says you keep making the leap over and over. I hoped I could. But there it was again, the yawning abyss.

And always now the tantalizing idea of marriage to this Continental playwright-translator. It could be as unconventional as he wished. In fact the prospect of an unconventional union appealed to me enormously. But his resistance and my insistence led to an inevitable ultimatum. Fritz called my bluff and left me. He moved out and into a small place on Horatio Street. I still heard from him periodically. Nineteen sixty-three staggered along, fraught with attempts on my part at reconciliation. In the early summer of 1963 I countered by leaving us both. I went away, home to Minnesota, still thinking that after a period of absence, Fritz would change his mind. I returned to find that he had changed his mind, all right. He had found a new girlfriend. Several years his senior, Gina was part Italian, part German Jew, a former mistress of Hugo's, his chief opponent in chess, a fact in which I found a dark significance. She was, in every physical attribute, my exact opposite. Where I was tall, she was short; where I was thin, she was thick; where I was blond, she was brunette. It didn't occur to me that other dichotomies were possible: perhaps where I was shallow, the new woman was deep; perhaps where I was neurotic and needy, the other was secure and independent. And it was not fair either that the new woman was a better cook.

By August I decided on an escape to Europe. Making it plain he would be traveling without Gina, Fritz said that he, too, would be in Europe then—making the trip we had talked so many times of taking together. He was enthusiastic about my plan. I would of course visit him at his father's house. (Fritz had made a kind of peace with his family by then.) I had their addresses. I had only to inform them of the date. I was expected.

My August visit to Germany was perverse, quixotic, willful, and above all irrational. Perhaps it is true that a woman in love is seldom a rational creature. I knew that Fritz, who would be in Hamburg, expected me to arrive via Madrid on the twenty-ninth. Instead I went to Copenhagen on the twenty-ninth. I told myself I did that because I had found it so hot in Spain, but was I giving myself an out in case Fritz—or was it I?—didn't want to reconcile? Better to miss the boat literally than through some deeper, more personal failure of my own. Still not cold enough in Denmark, I went on to Norway. I might yet have arrived within a reasonable approximation of the date I'd announced. Instead I opted for the train that went to Germany via the length of the coast of Sweden.

Years later, when people asked me why I wasn't married, I'd laugh and say, "It was too hot in Spain." They took it as a joke.

When I arrived in Germany at last, I called Hamburg, only to discover that Fritz, having concluded I was not coming, had struck out for Copenhagen in the family sailboat. He would return on roughly the date of my arrival back in New York. Beautiful. I could scarcely have missed it better.

I left the phone booth and inquired of the customs officer how to get to Niendorf, a nearby village where, I knew, Fritz's father had a house. One of the customs officers was just going off duty. He lived in Niendorf. Could he offer me a ride?

There was no mistaking the man who answered my knock. Herr Steffan-Freude was seventy-four and seven feet tall. His tanned face beamed down at me. He put one arm around my shoulder and with the other took my hand. "Janet, come in." I was surrounded by a gray suit of scratchy material, then encouraged down a short, narrow hallway and onto a blue couch in the living room.

"Now," said Fritz's father, calmly producing a decanter and glasses, "we will have a little sherry."

His English, while slow, was correct; he told me he had not spoken it since 1922, when he made an exhibition tour of the United States with a plane of his design, very advanced for those times. In the course of that tour, he told me, he had flown with his partner to Siberia and then the North Pole.

As I told him of *my* little trip, my mind checked off the things about the room that were already familiar to me. How proud Fritz had been that this house was designed by his father. Fritz had drawn it for me on a paper napkin in New York, even down to the French doors.

I recognized, too, the portrait of Frau Steffan-Freude over the dining room table. I had seen one photograph of Fritz's mother, taken in the conservatory of the big house in Wismar where they had lived from 1934 to 1944, though the lady herself had died in 1941. I would have known her from her eyes alone. They were Fritz's eyes.

We sat sipping sherry in the living room, which was strewn about with a widower's clutter of newspapers and books. I spotted an open volume of Goethe.

Herr Steffan-Freude smiled a charming smile at me. "Will you join me at my simple supper?" I protested that my heavy dining on the boat had left me not at all hungry. He said, "Keep me company, in any case." Moving to the table under the portrait, he held my chair for me. I saw that bread and cheese had been laid out.

Herr Steffan-Freude went to the kitchen and, moving with his slow, deliberate air, brought to the table a white china teapot. I offered to assist him. He refused with a wave of his hand. Soon he was seated beside me, and a mellow camaraderie fell over the table as we shared the bread and cheese, but not before Herr Steffan-Freude lifted a bottle of rum from the bookcase behind him. Holding it up, he said, "We will add a little rum to the tea this evening, in honor of your visit." And so we did, conversing on the topic that had been binding us together all along.

I asked him if he remembered a story Fritz told of himself as a four-year-old. He had slipped into the kitchen while the staff was engaged in preparing a large, festive dinner, stolen half a dozen tarts, and eaten them, every one. Later, when his mother came into the nursery to supervise her sons at their meal, she asked, "Fritzie, why are you not eating? Won't you have at least one bite?" Shoving away his plate of vegetables with a virtuous air, Fritz had cried, "No, no—it will make me fat."

Herr Steffan-Freude greeted my recital of this episode with laughter, yet with a certain restraint, as if he still found his son's behavior lacking in discipline.

I brought out some Swiss chocolate I'd purchased on the steamer, and we smiled at each other as it melted on our tongues.

Not long afterward, for we were both tired, I was shown to a bedroom to the left at the top of the stairs. I had no sooner settled into the bed than, engulfed by its red feather duvet, I fell into a deep sleep.

Next morning we breakfasted together, Herr Steffan-Freude allowing me to do dishes, though he rearranged everything after I had put them away. Then I watched, entranced, as he contrived to get his seven-foot frame into an old gray Volkswagen and we putted off to Travemünde, a very pretty resort town. Hundreds of sailboats of all sizes were moored alongside the large marina. A regatta was in progress. As we drove up a curved drive to stop before a huge white luxury hotel, Herr Steffan-Freude announced his intention of taking me to lunch.

In the hotel's grand, airy dining room, which was entirely deserted, tuxedoed waiters lurked behind every pillar. As Herr Steffan-Freude held the waiting armies at bay, we lunched on clear beef broth, tender golden fish, rice pilaf, and *Gurkensalat,* savoring a bottle of mellow Rhine wine and forming between us a friendly island of humanity in the ghostly atmosphere.

Just then, a wedding party emerged from the hotel and passed across the terrace to the lawn, where they posed for photographs, a handsome couple. The blond bride's white, full-skirted dress billowed out like a sail around her legs. It was a small party, only the two attendants, a set of parents, and a naughty young cousin in the group. The bride's shoe came off and the groom teased her, withholding it, now behind his back, now over his head, until she gave him a kiss and he tapped her lightly with it on the tip of her nose, then fell on his knees with exaggerated gallantry to slip it on her foot.

From the deserted dining room, the two of us watched all this in silence, absorbed in our own thoughts—perhaps a bit oppressed by our thoughts. Then, all at once, we pushed back our chairs and left the table and the hotel.

As we rolled back into the driveway of the sensible little house in Niendorf, we saw a big gray Mercedes pulled over on the lawn.

"Ach, wie schön," said Herr Steffan-Freude, "Karl and Lotte are here." This was Fritz's brother and his wife. I guessed that they must have driven up from Heidelberg, where Karl worked at the Max Planck Institute. The hall and living room became a jolly confusion of greetings and hugs, of questions and answers that changed places in midair and ended with everyone getting only the information they already knew.

Lotte and I were soon talking like long-lost friends. The two of us went upstairs to sort out baggage and closets and featherbeds. I crossed the hall to take a smaller upstairs room with more coat hangers. I let out a cry as I saw something gleam from between the covers of a book on the dresser: "Oh, but that's mine. How can it be mine? But it is my bookmark!" I held out the gold clip for Lotte to see my initial there. She laughed. "That's not so strange. Fritz was here for a day to pick up the boat. He must have left his things in this room."

Feeling a little faint at this discovery, I considered how I came to be in this little bedroom under the eaves in Niendorf, Germany, and how I came to be holding in my hand the copy of Henry James's *Portrait of a Lady* that I had last seen in my apartment in New York. Looking around the room more closely, I saw the gray-blue sweater, frayed at the elbows now, that I had given Fritz two Christmases ago, the first Christmas we were together. I saw the bronze and black striped tie I had given him on his birthday, and there were some familiar yellow fragments from his asthma pills, which followed him everywhere. The sound of voices downstairs stayed on the edge of my consciousness, but the sense of what was being said went past unheard as I stared at the pile of Fritz's manuscripts, which seemed, even more than his clothes, even more than my bookmark, to bring his presence home.

Then I was overtaken by the thoughts I had been shutting out ever since the moment of my arrival the day before. This was just the way it would have been. This was exactly the way it would have been if Fritz and I had come over for the wedding. Our wedding. The house full of people, the special fetes in my honor. The reception at the great hotel. The photographs on the lawn. The fatherly gallantry of Herr Steffan-Freude, the girlish confidences of Lotte in the upstairs bedroom. I would have recounted the family jokes I already knew, and they would have let me in on more. Fritz's things would have spilled over into the bedroom across from mine; there would have been sounds of laughter floating up the narrow stair. It was all just the way I had imagined it a hundred times. But I was not here for a wedding. There wasn't going to be any wedding. And Fritz was heading, it was thought, for Copenhagen.

Where had I gotten the idea that we were going to be married?

Just because, for months and months, and even years, we had been inseparable. I had thought, I had really thought, that when he protested against it, he was jesting. It was a joke between us that whenever he was particularly delighted by me, some piece of foolishness of mine, he would pull up short, his face still wreathed in smiles, hold up a finger, and growl, "*but,* I am not going to marry you." It was the same joke, a variant reading, of his loving me and whispering, "Don't get the idea into your head that I love you." Or again, when we had been away from each other and I ran up to him, he would whirl me around until I came to rest under his chin, look down at me, and say, "Nevertheless, you are not to think I am going to marry you," and plant a husbandly kiss on my forehead. I took all these things as certainties of their opposite. It was a fatal holdover of believing in popular songs. "If I loved you," "Don't throw bouquets at me," "I'm not a bit in love," the lovers would sing. Even Shakespeare lent weight to the argument "[The gentleman] doth protest too much, methinks."

And so I had gone on happily believing, all Fritz's protestations to the contrary, until my remarks so openly betrayed my line of thinking that Fritz felt compelled to speak seriously to me. He had not taken that view of the course his life was to follow, he told me. He could not. He was a poet. That was gloomy, lonely work. His stance must be one of opposition. His stance must be that of a man alone. There was no place in that view for a passionate young bride. I pointed out to him that he had been a poet all the while we had been together and it had not prevented him from writing a play during that time.

"Don't you want to have children?" I asked.

"You forget. I have a child, a daughter in Hamburg. And you see that I did not marry her mother. Nor did she wish to marry me. Women think differently about these things in Europe. We have a business arrangement. I pay for the expenses of the child. She goes on with her life."

Robbed of my last, best argument, I had pulled back then. Finally I had cried and shouted at him that he had ruined my life and that I never wanted to see him again. He had remained serious even in the face of my tears, something he had always refused to do. That was what had convinced me. He had said, "I am so sorry, Janet. I did not want to hurt you. You are such a wonderful girl." And then he left.

So what was I doing, standing in this bedroom in his father's house? What in hell was I doing here?

ONE FINE DAY ABOUT a month after my return from this debacle, I answered a knock on my door. Gina and Fritz were standing there. Gina, looking older and a thousand times more self-possessed than I, offered her hand in the European way of greeting.

"We've come for my things," Fritz said, handing over his set of keys.

My face twisted into a shape I had read about called a grimace. A sort of strangled voice issued from my gargoyle mouth: "You break my heart into a million pieces and now you want to shatter it some more by coming in here with *her*"—here I looked daggers at Gina—"to pick up some miserable sweater or book or something?"

Fritz stood his ground. "Well, yes."

I crumpled onto the top step of the hall staircase. Sweeping a backward hand, I croaked, "Go ahead then, but don't expect me to help."

The two of them went in, and I could hear them moving about, filling the soft-sided canvas bag Fritz had brought along. Ten or fifteen minutes later they emerged, the canvas carrier round with contents, a filet bag of things swinging from Gina's hand. I stood, pushing my back against the wall to let them pass. Gina murmured something that may have been "Sorry to trouble you." Wronged and righteous, I said nothing. Their footsteps sounded loud on the stairs—small wonder, laden as they were. After a while I went into the apartment and looked around. Not a lot had been taken, but it felt like more.

A World Awry

I was in the discount drugstore buying a carton of Kents on my lunch hour when I heard about President Kennedy's being shot in Dallas. Hurrying back to the eighteenth-floor desk as to a bunker, I soon learned there had been no mistake. The sequence of events for the rest of that ghastly weekend is hazy, but I do remember that I had a date that Saturday night with a wonderful guy I knew from my church, Saint Peter's. I will call him Stan Johnson. We came back to my apartment after a somber pizza somewhere in the Village. People all but embraced perfect strangers on the street, so hungry were we all for consolation. Up at my place, Stan asked me so sweetly to "let my hair down" that I did. Never happened before. But there we were, me lying fully clothed on top of his chastely covered form, a foot-long swath of blond hair swinging all around us. He didn't say a thing. Just ran his fingers through it over and over, a look of sheer rapture on his face. No, we did not go to bed, nor do any other thing. The next day, after church, I met him again, and he asked me up to his apartment so we could watch television (I did not own a set). We watched with disbelief as Ruby shot Oswald. I had to break away then, to go home and call my folks.

At noon on Monday I joined a massive turnout at Fifth Avenue Presbyterian on Fifty-Fifth Street. The service ended with everybody saying the Lord's Prayer in unison, and I found myself somehow more moved by the men whose faces streamed tears than by us females, who knew more about public displays of emotion. On my way home from work I purchased a small television so as to fully participate in what I knew was my first wartime experience. What war? Who was the enemy? I didn't know, but I did know that my life as an American would never be the same.

Through the violence that marked the years between Dallas and our final departure from Vietnam, the magazine and my protected spot at it began to feel less and less protected. There was theft on the editorial floors. Sam the shoeshine man was no longer able to get access and offer in situ shines. The sandwich cart from the lobby shop was barred. My desk was moved from its spot near the back staircase to a closed and windowed booth out by the elevators. All people with business on eighteen, and even those with offices there, had to be cleared and buzzed through locked doors by me.

Everywhere in the country, from the stage at Carnegie Hall to the streets of Selma, exploded with new and violent sights and sounds. Pop culture, too, reflected upheaval. The pulse of rock and roll was being felt, even by the likes of me. I was given a comp ticket to Bob Dylan's first concert at Carnegie Hall. I thought that he was a nasal-voiced screecher with a harmonica in his mouth, that he looked as if he was in need of a bath, and that the fuss being made over him was a joke at the expense of the over-thirty crowd. But I had to admit that when he sang "The Times They Are A-Changin'," he was onto something. And when he screamed, "But you don't know what it is / Do you, Mister Jones?" I could relate.

Meanwhile, back at the office, I began to realize that my own political views were on occasion beginning to diverge from those of the leftists around the magazine. I had mixed feelings about abortion, for example. I had no quarrel with "a woman's right to choose," or with the idea that a woman should have sovereignty over her own body (never mind that I had ceded my own to Marco, the doctor). What was bothering me was the indifference I thought radical feminists displayed to the moral consequences of abortion as a form of birth control. It seemed to me they gave little or no thought to the hardening effect on poor minority women being forced to use it that way. Weren't they the very members of society the Far Right would condemn to giving birth to "welfare and crack babies"? Surely sex ed and planned parenthood was the better way to go. I once tried to argue this over lunch with the feminist rock critic for *The New Yorker,* Ellen Willis. Maybe I'd have gained some credibility if I'd come clean about my own past. As it was, I could see she didn't pay me much mind. And having put my case so badly and so dishonestly, I couldn't blame her.

Largely apolitical in the years with Harold Ross, the magazine had taken on a definite liberal bias under William Shawn, most of which I could applaud. On environmental issues, Rachel Carson's *Silent Spring* first appeared in its pages, as did articles of concern about the health hazards of tobacco and asbestos and about nuclear waste. The complete separation of the business and editorial departments placed *The New Yorker* above some of the pressures felt by other magazines, which feared the loss of advertising revenue. Actually, Monsanto did withdraw its advertising after the Carson piece ran, and the magazine itself began to refuse cigarette ads in 1964. On a less lofty note, a policy of no ads for "foundation garments" or underwear of any sort had gone into effect the year before. Still, one could see plenty of ads for luxury items like high-end clothing and jewelry. Such ads, running alongside James Baldwin's fiery essay on racial oppression "Letter from a Region in My Mind," struck some readers, as well as some of us in the editorial department, as a case of strange bedfellows. The Rovere Letter from Washington, too, regularly pissed off Republican readers, who may have had to decide between Senator Joe McCarthy, whom Rovere nailed early as a demagogue, and their fondness for *New Yorker* cartoons.

In spite of this distinctly liberal editorial slant, *The New Yorker*'s only overt editorial opinion was confined to the front of the Talk of the Town section under Notes and Comment, where political opinion ran heavily in favor of Democrats, the Kennedy presidency, and the civil rights legislation of Lyndon Johnson. That changed as the column tilted against LBJ's ill-fated support of the war in Vietnam. Richard Nixon, who had already gotten into the editors' bad books when he went after a longtime friend of the magazine, Alger Hiss, came in for harsh criticism, particularly when he ordered the incursion into Laos. Jonathan Schell, a reporter new on the roster, whose "Village of Ben Suc" savaged the "we had to destroy the village to save it" mentality of the hawks, became Mr. Shawn's writer of choice for the antiwar Comment pieces. Jonathan came down and worked in a vacant office on eighteen, where Mr. Shawn often joined him to go over the copy as Friday night deadlines neared.

In my own way I was trying to sort through the new scene brought about not only by the abortion discussion but by the arrival of the pill and the sexual revolution itself. In this I welcomed the views of one of the cartoonists on my floor. Warren Miller was a tall, jovial midwesterner whose cheery visage didn't fool me. I was a midwesterner myself, and I knew that the face we feel it necessary to show the world can hide a bushel of unease. In Warren's case, I suspected, it was the knowledge that he, as a graduate of Beloit College in Wisconsin, was not going to cut much ice in the snooty land of slick eastern Ivies. Yet the guys in the art meeting all seemed to appreciate the wry cartoons Warren turned out. They were done in bold india-ink brushstrokes of a skill and craft that didn't seem shy at all. Warren and I shared a brief season of friendly dating. We found it relaxing, over dry martinis and bloody steaks at cool Village spots, to admit to each other that the singles bar scene scared us silly.

One Friday after work, Warren and I were having a drink in the back room of an Eighth Avenue bar known to be a press hangout. We ran across Thomas Meehan, who waved us over to his booth to meet his date. Tom had recently scored a big hit with a piece that ran in the magazine as a "casual," the preferred name for the short, humorous pieces that are today called Shouts and Murmurs. It was a hilarious riff on people in public life whose first names were made up of two syllables, two or more vowels, and a consonant—Abba Eban, Uta Hagen, Yma Sumac, and so forth. Tom posited a delightful fantasy cocktail party at which he was expected to perform the introductions. "Abba, Eva, Eva, Abba, Eva, Uta, Uta, Eva, Eva, Yma"—you get the picture. It set his career on fire. Soon he was to leave the magazine to write for the television show *That Was the Week That Was.* He went on to become a Broadway Tony winner, writing, among other hit shows, the books for *Annie* and *The Producers.* Tom's date, a smiling brunette, was having her own success as a result of passing herself off for ninety days as a Playboy Bunny and writing about it for the glossy new magazine *Show.* That publication died an early death, but *Ms.*, the feminist magazine she started, had better luck and a longer run. Gloria Steinem was her name.

About this time I got invited to a rally for Bobby Kennedy at the Roosevelt Hotel. The candidate himself was introduced by Rose Kennedy, who got huge laughs by quipping about the toilet-training habits of Bobby as a toddler. When he took the mike from her, the soon-to-be senator from New York scored laughs almost as big by thanking his mother for her "shy and tender" introduction.

All in all, there was little doubt which side the majority of us voted with, but still a semblance of political neutrality was encouraged at *The New Yorker.* This did not prevent a bunch of us from attending another campaign event in 1968. Rick Hertzberg, Tony Hiss, George W. S. Trow, and Jake Brackman—in other words, the young Turks—announced they were all going over to snicker at George Wallace from a press table to which they'd finagled passes at the fund raiser Wallace was holding at the Hilton. Rick invited me to come along. Once there, I felt comfortable enough with this pack of "kid brothers" from the magazine, but less so when we were joined by Norman Mailer and Jimmy Breslin. I remember no other woman at the table, and I sought a low profile by slouching in my seat and summoning a second drink to hide my confusion. Mailer, Breslin, and a majority of the others were soon way ahead of me, drinkwise and otherwise, and serenely untroubled by the skirt in their midst. Snickers and zingers flew around in fine fashion but were destined never to see the light of print, as the next day in Maryland some nut with a gun shot at the governor, and his bullets put the candidate in a wheelchair for life.

A New Roommate

Andy Logan was responsible for my one intimate experience with a person of color. Andy was the magazine's reporter on city hall. She was held in such respect in the pressroom downtown that it almost rose to fear on the part of the other newsmen and -women. (There were far fewer of the latter—Andy was as singular a figure there as Rosalind Russell was in *His Girl Friday.*) In the office, she was a down-to-earth presence, a small woman with short brown hair and straight bangs. In addition to writing a column in *The New Yorker*'s back pages nearly every week, Andy was a wife and mother. How she did all this, and juggled two households—an apartment in town and a house on Fire Island—I cannot imagine. A Swarthmore graduate and a die-hard liberal, Andy was always looking out for the underdog. She was keen on winning recognition for the magazine's Talk of the Town reporters. Through the end of William Shawn's tenure, their pieces always appeared unsigned. Andy would find their identities (wrested from a reluctant production department) and post the Talk galleys—writers' names added in Andy's bold hand—on the editorial office bulletin boards. It was a measure of her clout that this gesture of protest was never interfered with.

Sometime in early autumn of 1964, Andy posted a notice on the eighteenth-floor board explaining that a young employee was urgently seeking new housing. The apartment she had been living in up in the Bronx had been broken into. It was deemed unsafe for her to return. So I gained a new roommate.

Sara Mitchell, a beautiful, nineteen-year-old African American, brought her possessions down to my place on West Twelfth Street the evening of the same day the notice went up. Sara, who had grown up just outside Macon, Georgia, lived with me through the winter of 1964 and on into the spring and summer of 1965. We were both small-town girls and churchgoers, so we had a lot in common, and we shared almost everything in those months, from cleaning and cooking to our thoughts on the universe. Most importantly, Sara shared with me her opinions about white people. They were opinions she held in common, she was convinced, with most people of color. She voiced them with a candor and a trust I had not been accustomed to from any but my most intimate white friends. And then she went on to do the same with her opinions of black people. If I knew anything about the state of race relations in America then, I owed it all to the months I lived with Sara.

I never had the heart to use the little back closet I'd reserved for Fritz, so there was no problem finding room for Sara's clothes. There were so few of them that they scarcely made a dent. Sara had four dresses, all cut from the same sleeveless, narrow-waisted, dirndl-skirted pattern she had sewn herself. They were all of cotton—one yellow, one work-shirt blue, one pink, and one a floral print with large red-and-black poppies on a white background. For the oncoming chill days of autumn she had a navy pleated skirt and a white blouse, over which she wore a light gray cardigan. I discovered that Sara had only two changes of underwear and stockings, which she hand-washed, along with a white cotton nightgown, every other day. One pair of two-inch heels and one pair of white sandals resided next to a pair of blue cotton mules on the closet floor. A tan raincoat and a navy polka-dot scarf completed the whole wardrobe. We had a harder time finding space in the minuscule bathroom for her considerable personal hair and skin products, until we hung a small four-shelf rack on the wall over the commode. A similar arrangement—new shelves mounted over the sink—was necessary for the storage of her vegetarian products in the kitchen, mostly health foods and herbal teas.

Always clean and neat, her slender figure and lovely features meant that Sara looked sweet whatever she wore. Her hair and nails and all the details of her person were healthy, gleaming, and fastidiously kept. I did not live in her presence for long before I learned there was no mystery about it—they were looks achieved by daily and nightly rituals of personal care. And while Sara washed, or ironed, or manicured or pedicured, or applied straightener to her hair, or otherwise busied herself in her amazing regimen, she made great conversation. A steady stream of softly accented talk came out of her mouth. She made no bones about the seriousness with which she took the way she presented herself to the world. She explained that it was a matter of black pride, to put to shame with the expedient of her own example any white prejudice she might encounter about black stereotypes.

Before we got very far along in the months we roomed together, Sara told me about the break-in up in the Bronx that had been the reason for our arrangement in the first place.

"I was just sitting on the bed in my little Bronx bedroom, taking off my shoes and thinking what was I going to do next, when this big dude with strung-out-looking eyes threw up the window on my fire escape—just as easy as if it had no locks on it at all—and stepped right in and started to tell me how I 'better not make no noise' or he would make me 'sorry for sure.'"

"So what did you do?"

"I just kept talking to him, soft and soothing, as if I thought it was natural as could be that he'd come in to see me like that, and like I had no idea he would wish to harm me. Said I could very likely be happy to entertain the thought of sleeping with a good-looking fellow like him as soon as we got to know each other. Said he should just go ahead and tell me about himself. Was he from a big family? and all like that. How many brothers did he have? And did he have sisters about my age? I thought I'd give him a scare saying I was just sixteen."

"My goodness," I said. "And what *did* he tell you about himself?"

"Oh, he had the usual sad story," Sara went on matter-of-factly. "Mother using, had five kids by five fathers. If any of the fathers stayed around, they mostly did it to beat up the kids or the mom."

"Did he seem to be sober?" I asked, thinking of my own dad's struggles with alcoholism.

"Dunno," said Sara. "I think it more likely he was a user and was coming down from a fix. Probably I would have had no luck with my grand plan otherwise. Actually it was lucky it did work 'cause it was the only plan I had. Mama always used to tell my sister and me"—and here she lapsed into what must be the way her mama had sounded when she was living at home in Georgia—"'Nobody gonna harm you if you can just make 'em remember they a human bein'.

You got to treat 'em like one and that's how you remind 'em they is one. Some poor souls ain't never *had* that experience. It throws 'em off their sinful course.'"

"And did it with him?" I asked. "Did it . . . er . . . throw him off his sinful course?"

"For a time. I can't say it would have been any use in the long run, but it kept him quiet and sitting on the bed and talking until Jamal—that's this Nation of Islam brother I've been going out with—came by and hauled him out by his collar. Then we got out of there right away and Jamal made me promise I'd get another place to live."

I had not heard of the Nation of Islam until the year before, when I'd read an article on Elijah Muhammad.

But Sara said lately a younger spokesman for the Nation who called himself Malcolm X was the one Jamal followed. "Jamal said he'd be by for me about seven thirty. You can meet him for yourself."

"Oh, that'll be great," I said, maybe a bit faintheartedly, as I was just then realizing that this little white corner of the West Village was going to be integrated whether my neighbors were ready or not.

It soon became clear that in my cool, hip building, some were not ready. Thomas Boggs was a case in point. He was a small-time accountant who lived in the one-room with a Pullman kitchen just opposite mine. We had become friendly enough that he introduced me to his sleep-over-every-other-weekend girlfriend, Margie. But that night Tom opened his door, found Jamal and Sara sitting on the top step chatting, and flipped out. Actually he said nothing in the presence of Jamal, but the next day he accosted me as I left for the office and reamed me out. He accused me of ruining the neighborhood and endangering the life of everybody in it.

That night I got home to find a note pinned to my door that said in big, shaky block letters FUCK YOU SALT & PEPPER. Sara was not surprised. She got a kick out of me—Pollyanna, namby-pamby me—calling him up and, when he answered, giving him my version of a telling-off. "Oh, Boggs, I know that was you. Just go soak your head!" Well, the notes stopped. But in deference to Boggs's nerves, Sara stopped holding conversations with Jamal and his pals out on the stairs. Instead she brought them in and they hung out in the living room.

One Saturday night my brother was in town from California and we stayed in for dinner. When Jamal came to pick up Sara, they accepted our invitation to join us. Of course, being Muslim, Jamal didn't drink, so he refused the wine, and Sara didn't drink anyway, and neither of them, being vegetarian, went in for the pot roast I had prepared, with its beef juices over everything. But they seemed fine with carrot sticks and fruit juice, and we all grew very companionable. Sitting around the table afterward, Jamal told a story about having to watch a shipmate drown and almost drowning himself in a storm off the Florida coast one time when he was working the shrimp boats. Grabbing our attention from the first moment, Jamal, it soon became clear, knew just as well as Sara how to tell a story.

"Me and Jorge were the only ones didn't go down with the boat. We must have hung on to that little sliver of ship's planking for a day and a night. Finally, Jorge started to cry and tell me he was slipping. 'Help me, Himmy,' he cried over and over."

Here Jamal gave us each a long look. "My name was Jimmy then, and Himmy was what he called me. He was calling me for help until he went under."

"Did you try to catch hold of him?" Joe asked.

Jamal shook his head. "I knew if I did help him, we would both be lost. I have learned there was no sin in that—there is no sin in fighting for your own life. In fact, it is your duty."

He looked at each of us, and while it cost us something, each of us returned his gaze.

Shortly after that evening, on the twenty-first of February, 1965, Sara attended a Malcolm X meeting. She was in the fifth row of the auditorium, immediately in front of the stage and only feet away from Malcolm X, who was scheduled to speak and was making his way to the podium when he was shot and killed. Sara was traumatized by the gunfire and the ensuing pandemonium, in which the gunmen were able to escape.

When she got home, all she wanted to do was huddle under a comforter and drink tea. We said very little, she and I, but she gave me the impression that she thought some members of the Nation of Islam—with whom Malcolm had quarreled—were responsible.

The meeting was on a Sunday. Sara did not go in to work on Monday but was well enough to return to her desk on the twentieth floor by Wednesday. That night Mr. Shawn called and asked to speak to Sara. It seemed one of the reporters on twenty who knew she'd been at the meeting and seen the assassination firsthand had mentioned it to Mr. S. He asked her to write something about it for the Talk of the Town. She did write a brief account of the event and her reaction to it—about five hundred words—but it didn't run, perhaps because she was too open with her suspicions of the likely perpetrators.

Sara and I went on as companionably as before, but the atmosphere in the city was tense in the aftermath, and Jamal and his friends no longer came as far south as West Twelfth.

Sara told me that the talk uptown was not for blaming, as she did, a rival black group, but rather for expressing certainty that Whitey, the Man, had done in Malcolm X. In fact, there was talk uptown, Sara said, that the lid was going to come off black anger, and the revolution would soon begin. Then, seeing my wide eyes, and perhaps bearing in mind my earlier confession that the only black people I saw, growing up, were in the movies, she patted my hand and laughed. "Don't you worry, honey. I'm going to tell them to spare *you*. You're OK."

By early summer, Sara was telling me, "Black folks get sunburned, too. Didn't you know that?" She showed me the inside of the back of her ears and the palms of her hands and the bottoms of her feet, which were lighter than the other parts of her. So we took turns rubbing sunscreen on hard-to-reach spots. Soon we moved from discussing Sara's skin to discussing skin in general.

Sara went on to conduct what I think of now as a crash course on race. She told me of the prejudice light-skinned black folks had against dark-complexioned ones. And she said nobody gave the brothers more bad rep and cut them less slack than other black people. Anytime I asked, I could learn from Sara some new class distinction practiced inside the black community.

"How come I never hear any of this stuff from Jervis [Anderson] or Charlayne [Hunter] or Sam [Harris]?" I asked one time, mentioning other African Americans on the magazine's staff. She put on her Georgia voice to answer: "They too well assimilated to talk black in front of you, hon. It's only because I'm a visitor up here in the North and you took me in, and I found in you a white sister who is a Christian I can trust, that I'm telling you these things. Also, don't believe it's love when brothers marry white women—it's color moving on up, that's what's behind it."

"Yeah, but"—I named a celebrity—"is married to a white guy—how about that?" I asked.

"She's moving up and he's making his guilty self feel more righteous," said Sara.

"Oh. I can't believe it isn't love, too, at least some of the time," I demurred.

Sara just looked at me and shook her head and laughed.

Maybe not all the things that Sara believed were right, but whatever she told me, she did truly believe, and I knew she made an exception to tell them to me.

By late March, Sara had stopped seeing Jamal and had begun to receive telephone calls and letters from an old beau in Macon. In May she went down to visit him. Not long after that, she wrote me that they were married, that she had started her own dressmaking-on-demand business, and that she was not going to be coming back. In July the following letter arrived.

Jan, Sweet One—

I've had so much to say that procrastination set in while I tried to determine how to say it . . .

If I touched the bottom of the creek, it would have to be admitted that your ex-roomie is less than content or thriving. On the surface of Lake-Loyalty-to-Marriage I could fake it and say that things are going along OK . . .

But that [they aren't] may be a good thing. Now I sort of HAVE to make the sewing business work.

I do hope to come up to N.Y. for a few days . . . When are you leaving for Europe? . . . If very, very soon, please call and let me know so that I won't have the shock of finding you . . . not There . . .

I MISS YOU—and hope that you're doing very well. You deserve good things from life—so keep on pushing.

With loving good wishes,
Sara

We stayed in touch through the next year or so, after which Sara left on a trip to India, and though I know she came back, several efforts to reach her in Georgia came up empty. I, too, hope she is doing very well. She deserves good things from life also.

Greece: The Journey Out

Søren Kierkegaard, the Christian existentialist, held great sway over me, being both Scandinavian and Lutheran. So when he described the search for one's true self as the primary task God sets us on earth, I took it seriously, all the more so since on that score I didn't have a clue. Sara always seemed to know who she was. I was muddled, not only about who I was, but about what kind of person that person was: Nice girl? Sexpot? Slut? Crazy lady? The options were not attractive. I took a big step toward solving my identity crisis on a trip to Greece in 1965; it began with a Eurail Pass shuffle across the Mediterranean and wound up in Brindisi on the SS *Carina,* a night ferry to Piraeus.

I was one of only a few Americans aboard. Along with some English families and twenty or thirty Greeks, we circled like so many negatively charged ions around a nucleus of French nuns, priests, and students—participants in a national "renewal" movement they called L'Homme Nouveau.

Up on deck, I leaned on the railing and stared at the ship's wake, wishing I could connect—fragments of myself, fragments of poetry.

The line from Homer, for instance, about the "wine-dark sea." Suddenly an elfin man in glasses and a green suit appeared at my elbow. Lifting an imaginary hat, he said in excellent French, "Bon soir, mademoiselle, je m'appelle Aristotle Caryannis."

Aha, I thought, *a Greek! Perhaps he can flesh out the line from Homer for me.* But Monsieur Caryannis did not recognize his poet in English, or in French either. The latter was not surprising, since the best I could manage was "la mer qui est la couleur d'un verre de vin," which had the unfortunate effect of encouraging him to go on talking to me in French, with a little English and German thrown in. He would speak, he said, of Prometheus and Christ: "A story philosophers tell." It was the story of the creation of the world. Here came the fishes, *poissons, Fische, beaucoup, beaucoup, beaucoup* . . . The moon was up. Monsieur Caryannis's spectacles caught the light. It was the sort of moon—neither full nor new—that nobody dwells on, but seeing it broke my concentration and I lost what slender hold I had upon the narrative thread. Suddenly there was a camel, a *dromadaire* bemoaning his small hump—or was it his inadequate organ? I scarcely knew anymore what was being related. A religious parable? A sex joke? All I found it possible to do was to smile blankly until Monsieur Caryannis left me for his dinner.

It turned out that he was only the first of many would-be suitors I encountered on this trip. Mr. Phillip, first mate, was next. He spoke to me in English in the polite form—a form that, as far as I knew, didn't exist. He told me that his four-to-eight watch was over, and while he had already dined, "If the young lady would be so kind as to accompany me to the bar, I would be pleased to present her with a whiskey and soda. There will be no charge." Sounded OK by me.

As we were finishing our drinks, he asked, "Has the young lady from America ever seen the sunrise at sea?"

I admitted that I had not.

"She will find it most agreeable," said Mr. Phillip. "I will call for her at five o'clock." He touched his cap and went off, presumably to attend to the social needs of the other passengers. I wondered why I hadn't declined, then shrugged and thought, *Why not?* The sun *would* rise, and I *would* find it agreeable to see it do so at sea.

I got a sandwich at the buffet and took a book to the drafty port side of C deck. The airplane-style reclining chairs were lined up four abreast on either side of a narrow aisle in twenty rows. I chose one in lieu of the cabin I couldn't afford. After a while my book fell limp in my lap and I began to dream. The boy was standing in a garden, pixie eyes sweetening the grave expression on his seven-year-old face. I had seen this child once, for a fleeting moment, in a photograph. It was Fritz as a child, and he had shown it to me when we were still living together. The boy had become my dream son, and in my dream we were a family. Fritz and I were married. We had a car. An ordinary, not new, family-type car, a Volvo. And he and I and our dream son were taking a Sunday drive, heading north on the Henry Hudson Parkway.

I was jolted awake by the touch of a hand on my thigh. I turned my head and saw Monsieur Caryannis's spectacles glinting at me in the dim light of the SORTIE sign.

"I thought you had taken a cabin," I said in icy German. To my mind this was a stinging rebuke that any right-thinking gentleman would take to mean "Get your hand the hell off my thigh and make yourself scarce." But it did not have this effect.

"Madame Caryannis was not feeling well, and as there was a lady who wished to share, I gave up my space to her," he explained.

"That was very considerate of you," I spat out, removing Monsieur Caryannis's hand to his own thigh.

He had begun to look very meek, almost stricken.

"I myself am feeling a slight chill," I added in a mellower tone. "If you will excuse me, I'll try to find a chair out of the draft." I moved to the seat farthest away. When I glanced back, he was still hunched rather forlornly over the chair I had left. I thought, *It is so easy to make a man ridiculous. One has only to say no. I suppose that's why they hate us so.* Now, gloomily, I began to feel guilt.

I must have dozed off, for the next hand on me was shaking me roughly by the shoulder. When I opened my eyes, Mr. Phillip was already vanishing. I ascended to the bridge through the grayness of slumbering bodies billowing over a cold sea.

A large wheel dominated the windowed enclosure. A hatless man in dark clothes stood behind it, feet wide apart. A steward handed around thick white cups of thick black coffee. I stood beside Mr. Phillip, looking out the window and sipping the sweet Turkish brew. Dark islands hulked all around us. Patras was to the right; Corfu, to the left and almost out of sight behind us. Somewhere up ahead a light was blinking. There was some pink behind the charcoal hump to the left of us. How could the sun come up to the left of us? Mr. Phillip would explain. He gestured to the chart room just behind the man at the helm. New, specific instruments of ancient design gleamed out at me from various points around the walls. A large, sturdy table held an orderly profusion of navigational maps. I bent over them with serious eyes, but the neat lines before me remained a mystery.

Then there was nothing to look at but the face of Mr. Phillip. It had deep lines, none of which signified anxiety. There were weather lines, squint lines, interrupted-sleep lines. They charted a handsome, seafaring course across straight features, around deep-set eyes. There was a flash of gold tooth in his smile as he brought his face down to mine. But his kiss was not kind. It was not even personal, and its urgency bore the pressure of haste rather than emotion. I broke away, with difficulty, and was propelled by my own momentum back into the other room. I subsided against the wall, breathing heavily.

The man at the wheel grinned. "Americano?" he asked. How could I make him understand that my flight had been motivated by hedonism, not puritanism? I liked to be kindly kissed.

"Mr. Phillip," he said, "is a good man. A very good man. I personally have never known him to be so moved by a beautiful woman as he has today shown himself to be." *Oh, brother,* I thought. Mr. Phillip entered the room. No one spoke. I moved out of the enclosure onto the port-side bow. Mr. Phillip followed. His arms encircled the part of the rail against which I was standing, then dropped to his sides as two kerchiefed ladies in mackintoshes popped up from behind the small foghorn.

"Le soleil est très joli, n'est-ce pas?" the first head-scarfed lady asserted. Mr. Phillip bowed his assent. A mustachioed German bearing a telescope emerged from the wheelhouse, muttered, "Guten Morgen," and stepped carefully over the sill. There was an exchange of guttural formalities. Suddenly Mr. Phillip herded us all back into the wheelhouse and I had a vision of him stuffing us, mackintoshes, head scarves, telescopes, and all, into his bunk for a whirlwind orgy. But he did not stop until we were all through the wheelhouse and out the other side. A whoosh of sudsy water explained the maneuver. The decks were being washed down. The sun had blazed into brightness, obscuring itself.

I went to the saloon and fell asleep in a deep red chair under a picture of Delphi. Again I dreamed. I dreamed that Fritz was a potato. I was in the dream, too. And a knight in armor, who announced that he had come to woo me and to ask for my hand. But my potato-love said to him, "You will never win her. I will seduce her with my eyes." I awoke and, disturbed by the linguistic trick my subconscious had played on me, slept no more but spent the morning at the deep tile-lined tank euphemistically referred to as the swimming pool.

Lolling in a deck chair under the bright sky, I made the acquaintance of a couple of drab female members of L'Homme Nouveau. Francoise and Claudine were from Amiens and would be spending the rest of the summer at Delphi. I would like to have known more about the religious aspects of their movement, but again language proved a barrier. Would they attempt in Delphi a synthesis of the pagan and the Christian? The Roman and the Byzantine? Or perhaps they were simply taking advantage of group rates. A strikingly well-built youth of eighteen or nineteen came by in electric-blue swim trunks. He greeted Françoise and Claudine and introduced himself as Pierre. He said that he, too, was a member of L'Homme Nouveau. Sitting down beside me, Pierre quizzed me charmingly about America. He was especially curious about New York, and Indians, confiding at one point, "Les Apaches sont pour moi très sympathiques." When he couldn't persuade me to join him in the pool, he asked me to please hold his watch. Soon he was cavorting in the liveliest manner with a girl in a bright yellow bikini and bright yellow hair. In between the shrieks and splashing of a water fight, I heard her cry, "Mach meine Haare nicht nass!" So it seemed she was German and was not engaged in any attempted renewal of French Catholicism.

Twenty minutes later the pair were still happily submerged, and I had tired of watch-sitting duty. I deposited the watch with Françoise and Claudine, reflecting that "L'Homme Nouveau"—the new man—was, to all intents and purposes, not so very different from the old.

At noon the *Carina* passed through the Corinth Canal. The delicate maneuver executed, the canal lined out behind us like a perfect punctuation mark—a dash of brilliant green leading to the next, and last, phase of our journey, through Greek waters to Piraeus.

BY MIDAFTERNOON I WAS jouncing my way into Athens on the seat of an uncertainly sprung city bus. Suddenly, through the grimy window on my left, I glimpsed the Parthenon and it hit me that I was truly in Greece. The bandage around my heart loosened. I got off at Síntagma Square and crossed to the sprawling café outside the American Express. It was siesta time and the plaza was full of young coffee drinkers, scornful of sleep, even in the midday heat. I saw two who smiled at me. I realized that I was smiling already. I was happy to be in Greece and it showed. They offered me a chair and I took it. They told me that their names were Andre and Alex, but I didn't really care what their names were. I was flattered. I was fought over. Alex moved in. He moved me out, out of the plaza, bag and baggage, into his blue Saab automobile.

"We must first find you a place to stay," said Alex. "I know a fine old house here in the Pláka. That is what we call this area around the cathedral, you know. It's just here."

We went in. A large black-haired man with a black mustache came forward from the rear of the house. Introducing himself as Mr. Propopoulous, he showed me a big, squarish room, bright and clean, on the ground floor. In a moment it was settled. My bags were placed in the room and the key was deposited in my palm.

"Come," said Alex. "We just have time for a lemonade on Philopappos Hill—and your first good look at Athens."

I was guided into the Saab once more and was soon being driven past ancient spots.

"That is the Temple of Jupiter," said Alex. "And there is the prison cell where Socrates was kept until his suicide." We swept past the small grated opening in a crumbling old wall, up to a hill facing the Acropolis. Leaving the car, we walked into an open, vine-shaded terrace and listened for a while to the cicadas.

"They live only one summer, you know," said Alex. "When we hear them begin to sing, we say in Greece, 'Summer has begun.' And when they have laid their eggs, they die."

"How very sad," I said, suppressing a smile. I wondered if this was the way Alex really saw things or merely his idea of how to talk to a woman.

"Now I must go back to my shop. And you must sleep. At nine, I will call for you, and we will go to the most beautiful beach in the world. We will have dinner on the terrace and listen to the waves lapping against the shore."

Back in Andria House I discovered that I was very tired. Even so,

I was too surprised to sleep. Having spurned overtures all over Europe all summer long, I had not the faintest idea why I had encouraged this one myself.

If you don't know, then who's minding the store? I asked myself. I shuddered at the thought of all that undiscovered territory encased in my skull. How had I become such a stranger? It wasn't only that I was in a strange country. Being clueless about my own motives and feelings was a prevailing condition with me, thrown into relief by the fact that I was no longer surrounded by people who insisted they knew me. I thought of my uncle Bill, back in Iowa, sitting at supper one Sunday with the people most familiar to him in all the world. He had sat considering us—his wife, brother, sister-in-law, sisters, nephew, and niece—then suddenly asked, "Who are these people sitting here?" He spoke in a normal tone of voice and at first he seemed to be addressing the lamp in the middle of the dining room table. Then his eyes moved slowly over our faces once again. "I don't know you," he said. "I don't know a blamed one of you." Exhausted by the weight of this recollection—or just exhausted—I did, then, fall asleep.

That evening, I took more trouble getting myself ready than I had in a long while. Alex was late, but he was pleased by my looks, so I was pleased. We drove under the flood-lit Acropolis, across Athens, then out to a highway along the coast. Greek music flowed from the radio. I felt very well.

A number of cottages lined a small cove, and we turned in beside one of them, passing a uniformed guard at the gate, who waved us through. Alex brought us each a drink as we sat on the terrace and ordered dinner from a nearby caterer. A radio was playing American music of the forties—the big bands. Alex proposed the Greek toast, "Yasou!"

After dinner, we had coffee laced with brandy. Alex relaxed and was at his most extravagant then, making love to me. He compared me to Eve and said he was in paradise. The next minute he was spinning a desert fantasy out of *The Arabian Nights.* Then, as I lay watching in disbelief, he sprang off the couch and began to show off for me. Doing calisthenics and boasting of his athletic trophies and ribbons.

I was reminded of Fritz and of an evening party on Long Island, during one of the bad times. Fritz's play had just come back from his publisher in Germany with a rejection, and he was drinking more than was usual for him. He did not hold his liquor well. There were about a dozen people at the party in a beach house that belonged to a photographer named Harry, who specialized in moody shots for fashion magazines. Because someone had mentioned the Cassius Clay–Sonny Liston bout, Fritz and Harry had challenged one another to a boxing match.

Harry's girlfriend and I watched from a corner of the room as the two grown men staggered around the living room in swimming trunks, protecting their noses with Harry's sons' junior gloves, each bragging loudly that he would very soon knock the other down. One of them actually did get a bloody nose when he tripped over his own foot and, falling, bumped his face against the corner of an easy chair. I had wanted to shout, "Please don't!" *Please don't show us how like little boys you are. We don't want to see how vulnerable you are. We come to you for strength and protection. If you show that you are weak, like us, we are confronted in a way that you are not—no, you really are not, having on some level known it all along—that we are alone, that no one is safe, and that men and women can only cling to one another, suspended over the void.*

Alex may have seen that my eyes were wet, for he drew my head down on his shoulder and spoke tenderly to me. To weep, to be consoled, must have been what I wanted. Soon I was lighthearted again. Alex heard me laughing in the bath and came in to ask, "What's so funny?"

I waved a sponge at the steep-sided porcelain chair I was sitting in and hooted, "This isn't a bathtub; it's a throne!"

Alex was wounded. "Many tubs in Greece are of that style," he retorted with dignity. "To me it seems a very pleasing form. I see nothing funny about it." Later he wanted to comb my hair, or, as he said, "plot" it.

"Not *plot, plait.*"

"Yes, please." And then, holding up his handiwork: "*Plait.* What a curious word."

"What a curious plait."

In the morning, as we drove back to Athens, Alex began worrying out loud that I was not seeing enough.

"You must go to one of our wonderful islands. You can go to Hydra in a day, simply by taking the tube from Omonoia Square right to the docks in Piraeus. And Hydra is magnificent."

I said I'd think about it, adding, "This evening, I want to go to the Sound and Light performance."

"An excellent idea," said Alex. He did not suggest going along.

We drew up in front of Andria House. Fat, dark, formal Mr. Propopoulous came forward, anxiously tossing his beads and crying,

"But where have you been? You did not come in all night." He looked past me at the street, where Alex was starting the Saab and pulling away from the curb. Mr. Propopoulous drew himself up into a semblance of a shrug and mumbled, "Ah, these young people . . ."

I DECIDED TO WASH my hair. Mr. Propopoulous was prevailed upon to put in motion a set of operations that eventually yielded hot water. When, hair washed, I expressed a wish to dry it and asked if he had a blow-dryer, Mr. Propopoulous pointed to the top of his house: "No such apparatus, but perhaps the sun?" Stepping out onto the roof, I was rewarded by a spectacular view, not only of the cathedral, but of a corner of the Acropolis as well, together with a vista of coral-tiled roofs and whitewashed buildings against a bowl of blue sky.

For long minutes I seemed to be in a world without activity. Even the sounds of the street were muted. Then, without warning, a window opened directly opposite me. A black-haired matron of thirty-five or forty appeared. Here, out of context, she seemed almost an apparition. *What can she be like?* I wondered. *Does she sing? What stories does she tell her children?* I wished I had learned the Greek word for "hello." Just as I was about to try out "buongiorno," the woman withdrew.

Reluctantly, as if it were something I had long avoided, I tried to think what the other woman had seen. I realized that I myself was more profoundly out of context, not only to this other woman, but to all who encountered me as I traveled about alone, possessed of no other identifiable relationship to the world or to society but a sexual one. Was it possible that I had no other identity?

That evening, as I walked up the steep path to the roped-off entrance of the Sound and Light show, people all around me were exchanging desultory comments in French. I turned to a buxom woman with a deep tan and sun-bleached auburn hair and ventured a question in French: "Excusez-moi. L'exhibition—ce n'est pas en anglais?"

The woman smiled at me: "Mais non, c'est en français, mademoiselle. Vous êtes americaine, n'est-ce pas?"

I admitted that I was and said I had come thinking that this performance was to be in English. Really, I was worried, I said. My French was not equal to the occasion. The woman smiled again and drew a handsome young man, also deeply tanned, into the circle of her arm. "Don't worry, mademoiselle. I am sure Pedro will be glad to be your interpreter, won't you, Pedro?"

Pedro grinned. "But of course, Mademoiselle—?"

"Groth."

"Mademoiselle Groth. I am Pierre LaSalle. These funny friends all call me Pedro. It is because I come from Nice. You must call me Pedro, too, and if I may, I shall call you—?"

"Janet."

"Jeanette, may I present to you our little group." He gestured at a group of people who might have stepped straight out of a Buñuel film. "Sylvie, Pepe, BaBa, Monsieur le Président, Monsieur le Docteur, Nikki, and Mr. Jacques. We are all traveling together, you see. We would be most happy if you would join us."

The others joined in the invitation: "Yes, by all means." "Do, please."

"Thank you—you are very kind."

The rope across the entrance was removed at this point and I followed the others to a row of folding chairs near the crest of the hill. Pedro and his "funny friends" had gone back to their conversation in French, and I was on my own.

Afterward, Pedro asked me to make myself a member of their party. I felt no great desire to join them, but Sylvie pressed me to come, giving me a strange look of desperation, and I relented. When we arrived, the Bacchus Tavern was very crowded, but after Nikki exchanged a few words with the headwaiter, we were assured the best table would be ours within minutes. So we stood in the roofless hall outside the vine-arbored dining room. Mr. Jacques, who had shown no interest in me before, suddenly struck a match and brought it up to my face. I saw his leering eyes behind the flame. Then he said in English, "First class. Absolutely first class."

The headwaiter came and seated us at a table near the front. When the food came, it was consumed without ceremony. More wine was poured. Everyone laughed a great deal. An ass wearing a wreath of vine leaves over his ears ate off the tables and pushed his head into the ladies' laps. At last, the rest of the party moved to go. Without seeing precisely how it had happened, I found myself alone in one of the cars with Pedro. He drove me to Andria House obediently enough but was less willing to let me leave the car and enter by myself. Caught in his vice-like grip, I laughed, releasing my breath in gasps that sounded almost like sobs. Pedro was passionately committed to possessing me; I, just as passionately to my release. To get his way, Pedro could only use force. To get mine, I resorted to feminine wiles. I seduced him into the idea of tomorrow. Tonight was impossible, I told him, with the perfect semblance of infinite regret. But tomorrow—ah, if he would only just be patient until tomorrow . . .

Finally a pact was sealed. I was to go into my hotel alone, since Pedro was convinced that I must. He would call for me in the morning and I would fly away with him. Inside Andria House, I informed Mr. Propopoulous that I would not be in to anyone named Pedro. It amused me to think of my seduction as a complete nonevent. Chances were, Pedro would not come. Most certainly, whether he came or not, I would not be there.

I left at seven for the boat to Hydra. But the boat to Hydra was not in port.

"It was full, so it left." That was the whole story. Departure time may be listed officially as 7:45 a.m. but if at 7:10 the ship is full, in Greece it is considered logical to cast off. I bowed before the logic of it, but I didn't know what my next move ought to be. I began to wander aimlessly along the wharf.

A number of small boats were taking passengers. I noticed one with the Arabic numerals 8:25 a.m. I couldn't make out its destination from the Cyrillic letters, but the sign below reading 18:45 must have been the return time. Just right. A day's journey to a Greek island was all I really wanted. I had no special brief to hold for Hydra. I went onboard. There was no sign of any other foreigner. When the little boat docked, the Greek passengers went to a walled church enclave where an outdoor bazaar was taking place in addition to the services inside. I was both too shy and too curious about the rest of the island to accompany them. Stopping at a roadside stand, I filled a net bag with some cheese, a bun, a container of yogurt, and three yellow peaches, then walked down what appeared to be the only road on the island.

Soon the shoreline became rougher, rising up from the water in steep banks. Gnarled trees and brambles made it difficult to get close to the water's edge. At last a narrow path led me to a rocky cove with a small, sandy beach where I could spread my towel. There I sat, watching the slither of a long, yellow-brown eel just below the surface of the water. *Now I've done it,* I thought. *Got myself into a situation where there is nothing to do but think.* Hardly knowing how, I set about some long-deferred self-examination. I wished, at last, to make sense of my life, the same life I had, on that night of the open gas jets in 1960, held forfeit to a passing mood of self-loathing. Oh, I had, in the Lenten season that followed, made my confession and set my soul in order, but now I tried for a more basic foundation. A return to my roots.

I began by taking a deep breath and looking around me. *Here I sit, in a quiet spot on an island off Piraeus whose name I do not know. No one in the world knows I am here. And no one in the world cares.* At this point, I brought myself up short. *That can't be true. No cheap self-dramatizing, please. My father and mother care. I care.* But on came the essential question: *Who am I? Surely the answer lies in the answer to the question, who are they? Think, girl. Think!*

Greece: The Journey In

I leaned back on my towel, closed my eyes, and thought. It was not for nothing that I'd been devouring *Bildungsromane* since the summer I was twelve and my older brother dared me to read the classics from his world-lit course. I knew one began these journeys with an overview of one's birthplace. There arose in my mind a picture of Saint Ansgar, Iowa, a farm community of fewer than a thousand people, dropped in a straight line down the map from Minneapolis and Saint Paul, to a point just below the Minnesota border. Mile upon mile of corn, soybeans, oats, and alfalfa stretched as far as my mind's eye could see. Every three or four of these checkerboard fields was punctuated by a grove of trees, sometimes poplar, more often scrub oak or pine, with a red or white barn, hugged on one corner by a silo, three or four sheds, and a white farmhouse, a pattern to be repeated until the horizon brought the sky down to a flat line miles away.

Towns dotted this farmscape—had to, to keep the farmers supplied, one or two villages to a county. The Mitchell County seat was Osage, twelve miles east, but Saint Ansgar was on a rail line, and the wagon trains of Swedish and Norwegian immigrants stopped there before dispersing west into Indian territory; it was a traffic hub and so the more colorful town. Still, there were no eighteenth floors in Saint Ansgar. The tallest structure, the grain elevator next to McKinley and Sons, was barely 150 feet high; the First Lutheran Parish House, however, rose an imposing two and a half stories on a large corner lot toward the north end of town.

The high-off-the-ground first floor became the site of church suppers. In the winters of my childhood these were often lutefisk suppers. I remember the smelly, frost-covered pails of lutefisk, soaking in lye and stacked in the vestibule of my father and mother's house. Mother would roll her eyes when she saw them coming. In vain she set bottles of Air Wick around the little hall. Still, the vestibule—and, if we were not careful to keep the door shut, the whole front of the house—stank to high heaven. On the day of the church supper my father and Uncle Bill would begin soaking off the lye and carrying the fifty pounds or so of now strangely flavored fish to the parish house to be served, swimming in butter, along with mounds of mashed potatoes. As if this were not starch and white food enough, the fish and potatoes were augmented by rolled crepe-like potato pancakes called lefse. The lefses, when smeared with butter and sugar, were quite tasty, and many a child, including me, passed over the fish to make a meal of them.

The dinner ended and the tables cleared, bedsheets were strung on clotheslines across one end of the hall to create a "fishing pond." We children would be allowed to "fish" by dropping light cane poles with string lines into the pond. Behind the sheets, stooping adults would tie a brightly wrapped gift to the end of the string and jerk on it until each child "landed" a toy. Always my favorite of the festivities. Saint Ansgar was also a place of German farmers, who, in addition to owning and operating the best farms in the state, had their own churches and church suppers. But I suppose you could say I wound up going to the Norwegian ones with the lutefisk and lefse because Daddy was a charmer.

The first picture of him in the family photo album shows Father looking pleased with himself, wearing a dark dress with a white lace collar and cuffs and long golden curls. There follows a photo of Father in a sailor suit. Next we get Father in side-buttoned knickerbockers, and then there is one of him in the doughboy uniform he wore, first at boot camp in the Ozarks and then, in November 1918, when he shipped out to France, arriving in Bordeaux just in time for the armistice. Then comes a baseball uniform from a year in Triple A. Then, having successfully negotiated "business college," Father joined a family partnership in his uncles' grocery store. His new life as a small-business man called for gabardine twill pants, a long-sleeved shirt and tie, and a big white apron. Its Groth Brothers Grocery logo, however, changed within the year. He and Uncle Bill bought out the uncles to become Groth Brothers Jack Sprat Grocery. A few years later, Father bought out Uncle Bill.

It was with the Jack Sprat franchise that Father met Mother, who caught his eye one day as she stood demonstrating pancake mix in the store's front window. She was fresh out of her two-year commercial degree at Wartburg College in Waverly, Iowa. Determined not to go back to the farm, where she would have been expected to rise at dawn and cook breakfast for twelve to fifteen men at threshing time, she—Esther Hartwig then—took a job as a traveling saleswoman in 1924. By the spring of 1925 she and Father wakened her sleeping parents, and as Grandmother and Grandfather Hartwig sat up in bed in their nightshirts, Father asked for her hand. The difference in their religion was noted and frowned upon as a serious obstacle. Father was, after all, a baptized, practicing member of the Norwegian Lutheran church; Mother, a member of the German Lutheran church, Missouri Synod. Two different kinds of Lutherans! Two different worlds! Permission to marry was granted, however, since Father was already an established merchant in the town.

In 1929, Father successfully negotiated for the purchase of a fine four-bedroom clapboard house, in which, seven years later, I was born.

My earliest memory is of Daddy reading "Bye, Baby Bunting" to me while in his and Mother's bed, me in my Dr. Denton's and he in his blue and white striped pajamas. While I heard about the rock-a-bye baby whose cradle might fall, I looked with fascination at a tiny red mole nestling among the thin, reddish-brown hairs on his chest. On his head, however, that red-brown hair—Mother would have said auburn—was thick and wavy, at least in the photographs of him in his youth. (He was already forty-three when I was born.) In infancy he wore a center part with big waves on either side swooping down toward his ears. I was startled to see a resemblance to the most often reproduced image of Oscar Wilde. There is one picture of Dad in his shirtsleeves, beside his Essex automobile, which captures the attractiveness he had to women. The center part is gone, thank God, and he seems to have brushed his hair straight back in a wavy pompadour. His left hand casually fondles the head of his German shepherd, Bruno, and he looks as if he could take on the world.

Here I pause to remind myself that I must not neglect the other half of my genetic makeup. Mother had a widow's peak and a heart-shaped face and looked ladylike and lovely in carefully chosen blouses and jewelry and well-cut suits. The way I remember her best is in a dark tailored short-sleeved dress with a white V-shaped collar, white gloves, and a picture hat. She looked like Irene Dunne in *Penny Serenade.* Men always showed special gallantry around my mother, and she always managed to accept their gallantries as nothing more than her due.

Counting the square footage of the deep, tree-shaded corner lot and the several outbuildings, the house I was born in was quite a spread. There were snowball bushes in front of the front porch, and Father was a proud tender of them. His other pride and joy was a picket fence and white trellis and archway between the flower garden that ran along one side of the house and the vegetable garden in the rear. He trained roses to grow up this archway, and one of my favorite photos is one he shot of Mother, my brother, and me standing there, in our ideal family mode.

Were we rich? I once asked mother, who said we were "comfortable," but added that nice people gave no thought to material things, treating all God's children, rich or poor, exactly the same. She had a fur coat, though, so we *looked* rich, although the coat was made of something called sable-dyed muskrat, which doesn't rise to the level of the best pelts. Still, she looked fine in it, especially with the little hats she wore on top, saucily tilted felt numbers with dotted veils.

Was I smug and satisfied as the princess of this castle? Not on your life. I longed for the family to move to the small white, green-shuttered bungalow in the next block, which looked more like the houses in my Dick and Jane books and spelled "normal" to me. The great cham of the frightened child. Let's be normal. Let's have no late-night fights or early-morning trips to Grandma's house. Let's have little squares of green lawn on either side of a cement walk leading up to the front door. Let's just hunker down and never have to overhear, from a sheltered spot under the counter at the Jack Sprat store, two women customers, as one says, "He drinks, you know. That's why she has to work. She thinks she can keep an eye on him." And the other says, "Yes, and where is he right this minute? In the tavern next door, I can guarantee it." Then the first: "Poor Esther." But I never told poor Esther what I heard. She knew it well enough. I have since identified the sick feeling of shame that washed over me when I heard those voices as the source of my lifelong timidity and what are now called "issues of self-esteem."

His athleticism notwithstanding, and probably as a consequence of the beer he consumed from his forties on, my father grew stout in middle age, which only made Mother call him "well fed" and even more distinguished looking. "Like a professor or a professional man," she insisted. But although for forty years he subscribed to a publication called the *Progressive Grocer,* Father was never what might be called a professional man. He was smart, and he was honest, and he was a good businessman, but as he had reason to know, that is not always enough in this world.

In point of fact, Father was several times close to utter defeat in his business and personal life. I suppose you could say, in the matter of the fire that destroyed the block of stores of which his Jack Sprat Grocery was one, that it was only one of the vicissitudes of fate. But if he had not been fuddled with drink on a two-week binge that fall, would he have failed to notice that the insurance had lapsed?

It was the week before Christmas when we were awakened by two sharp explosions, like shots out of a big hunting rifle. The whole sky was red orange, with black sparks shooting up into it, all visible out of the second-story bedroom where—as a temporary measure while my own bedroom was being painted—my cot stood in the corner opposite the big walnut bedstead where Mother and Daddy lay.

Daddy leaped out of bed, holding on to his pajama bottoms so they wouldn't fall down on account of his having broken the string. He held me back with a wave of his free hand, but his own face was close to the window and his voice anguished as he cried, "Oh God, Mother! It's the store! It's the store!" He pulled on some pants, a shirt, and shoes and ran out of the room and the house to rush uselessly to the scene. The whole block—the bakery next door, where the flour exploding had sparked the blaze, the grocery, the little blacksmith shop, and the corner beer parlor—all smoldered in black, evil-smelling swirls the next morning as Mother made me walk to school on the other side of the street. That was so I wouldn't see the hole in the ground, the cellar of the Jack Sprat, which was the only thing left of a property that, it became apparent, had been uninsured since September 15. The upshot was that he and Mother, whose principal asset it was, had to bear the entire loss themselves.

That was December 1945. Early in May 1946 we moved to Clarence, Iowa, another small town in the east-central part of the state—leaving my brother behind to finish his schooling. It was while going through the fourth and fifth grades in Clarence, light years away from New York, that I first set my heart on living in Manhattan. In Clarence, Mother and Father and I, with the aid of Bob, the projectionist, ran the town's only movie theater, the Roxy. Mother sold the tickets, Father took the tickets. I popped the corn.

My job operating the popcorn concession meant that I was at the movies seven days a week. Some of the films we showed in those postwar years were what are now called film noir, and they invariably opened with an aerial shot of the skyscrapers of Lower Manhattan. I didn't pay all that much attention to the plots of these movies, but I absorbed from them the conviction that life begins in New York City. Inwardly, psychologically, I was headed for New York from that time on.

Even by keeping the overhead to a minimum, business at the Roxy was poor—not because of television (still a decade ahead) but because the town was largely made up of conservative Methodists who did not hold with moviegoing. Unable to sell it as a theater, after less than two years Father swapped the building and the lot it stood on for a silver Airstream trailer. We hitched it to the family car, a gray 1945 Dodge, and took Route 66 to Long Beach, California, where I spent grades five (what there was left of it) and six on the West Coast. For a time, the sun of sunny California shone on the family fortunes, permitting my parents to own and operate, with the help of only skeleton staff, a diner and a short-order restaurant, directly opposite each other on the West Pacific Coast Highway. The way began to seem clear for us to move out of the trailer and, for the first time since Saint Ansgar, have a house of our own to live in.

There was just one fly in the ointment—the ointment itself: the beer on license in the short-order restaurant, and my father's fondness for it, and his weak head for tolerating it without loss of function. Mother enlisted my help in keeping the lid on Dad's intake, and between us we managed to keep it down to zero while he was under her eye or mine. But there were inevitable glitches, and one night one of them resulted in tragedy. A US Navy able-bodied seaman first class had been sideswiped, his motorcycle overturned, and the sailor's foot seriously injured. (He was later to lose a toe.) Passersby had gotten the license plate of the car that did not stop, which proved to be the 1945 Dodge registered to Dad. Awakened from a sound sleep, Dad was completely unaware that anything untoward had happened as he made his way home from a series of tavern visits. But that was of course no excuse. By the time the services of a good attorney were secured, a trial was held, jail time served, and damages and attorney fees paid, the sum total could only be managed by selling the trailer, selling the diner, selling the short-order restaurant, and asking Grandma Minnie to advance Mother's inheritance—most of the acreage of one of Grandma's five farms. None of this was enough to destroy his good standing in Great Hartwig's eyes, as her children and grandchildren called her, now that her offspring had reached a third generation. Both before and after the trial and the sentencing and the six-week incarceration in Los Angeles County Jail, she maintained, "Joe Groth is an honest man. I've always said so and I always will." Though she could be judgmental and often was, that sign of integrity was key to retaining her financial support.

Wiped out, we returned to the Midwest, and Mother and Dad bought a one-pump general store and gasoline franchise in Moscow, Minnesota, thirty miles or so north of Saint Ansgar. When I was twelve and we were living in Moscow, nature closed in on me. I got my first period, and Mother gave me the lecture about the birds and the bees. In her version, good Christian men and women "like your Dad and me" never had sex before marriage, and after marriage only when they wanted to have a baby. Because of the age difference between my brother and me, I thought there must have been a lot of holding back somewhere in there. I was sure I had discovered the real secret behind Father's alcohol addiction. He was sex starved, like George Brent in *Harriet Craig.* Or was it Wendell Corey?

In 1950 my parents sold the general store and bought a mom-and-pop grocery in nearby Austin, a town of twenty-six thousand. Austin was more or less owned by George A. Hormel and Company, whose main plant put out a number of tinned processed-meat products, the most famous of which was Spam. I hated Austin, hated the basketball-crazy Austin High School, hated the already established cliques that ran its social life. I longed even more for the day I could, like Gene Tierney in *Laura,* storm the canyons of New York. But at the time I was fourteen, fighting baby fat, pimples, and wallflower isolation at school dances. Suffering wave upon wave of self-doubt, I turned to my mother with a question the answer to which I dreaded and thought I already knew: "Mother, am I pretty?" After a careful pulling up to a stoplight—we were in the family Studebaker at the time—she said, "Why, honey, you're plenty pretty enough. You just need to stop spending all your time reading and get out more and make more friends." Mother was right. Still, I spent the next three years in an armchair with a book. I read Thomas Wolfe, Tolstoy and Dostoyevsky, Hemingway and Fitzgerald. Mother let slip one day, unaware that it could hurt my feelings, her opinion that reading books was "pretty much a waste of time."

I got the real story of her relations with Dad a couple of years after I'd moved to New York. I was on a visit back home and we had done our ritual shopping trip and lunch. Finally, after a rum Collins or two, Mother opened up and let it out that they had been "real sweethearts" to each other the whole of their married life. I gathered, by a little gentle probing, that this meant they had been sexually compatible and, well into their seventies, still enjoyed a before-sleep cuddle.

I found Mother's story that she and Dad had had a completely fulfilling marriage tough to swallow. Can you imagine? After all that cussing and door banging. After twisting myself into a pretzel lest I become what I had thought of as her Joan Crawford withholding-bitch self. It was only a figment of my imagination. Well, fiction would be neater, but truth compels me to tell it like it was.

So much for who they were and where I'd come from. Time for a look at who I was.

A nice-enough-looking American girl. Twenty-nine, medium blond hair with not much curl to it. Too thick in the nose for refinement of feature. A little too round of chin. But pleasant faced and happily proportioned. There were plenty of good reasons why I shouldn't have been, yet I was dissatisfied.

I had remained in thrall to that little red mole on Daddy's chest all my life. I was a daddy's girl who, when I grew up, did not know how to deal with men, did not know how to be honest about my emotions toward them or myself. By the time I got to college my head was full of an indigestible swirl of role models. Part of me yearned to be a kind of female Albert Camus. I envisioned myself in a trench coat with tough existential principles, an impeccable writing style, and an aura of modern saintliness that would keep Sartre and all would-be mockers in check. My female ideals were an incoherent mix of Lauren Bacall singing huskily and playing piano through cigarette smoke, Joan Leslie wearing puffed sleeves on the farm, and Ingrid Bergman being impossibly brave. One thing they all seemed to have in common was being in love with Humphrey Bogart, a man old enough to be Lauren Bacall's father—and mine. If I thought at all about who I was and who I wanted to be, I became resentful over the fact that the world didn't give a damn: it was going to define me superficially in any case. Yep, a dumb blond. That conviction got all mixed up with the idea of seeing males who were my contemporaries as predators on lovely young blonds like me. They were gauche, hot, ill-regulated, hormonally directed, vain creatures who would approach me relentlessly with no respect for my humanity, no ideas of love, romance, or marriage, but just the one thing on their minds. I dimly knew that men my own age had pimples, too, and were as hapless in their way as I, for which I found it difficult to forgive them.

In those first months when I lived in the city, I often "wandered lonely as a cloud"—with or without Wordsworth—in Central Park. I was, of course, hoping some man would approach and offer to cure me of my loneliness. But I never acknowledged that to myself, and when, over and over, a man would come up to me and make just such an offer, I was shocked and outraged. I remember one particularly nice-looking, slender lad, who said in halting English, "Excuse me. I am Yoel. I am an Israeli. And I would like to get to know you better. May I, please, know your phone number?" I had just been interviewed at CBS, where they had asked whether I could type, and lost interest when I said I could not, so, having it handy, I gave him the number of the Columbia Broadcasting System. Mean thing to do.

As I thought back on the confusion and lack of self-understanding that had pursued me my whole life, I could see that it had begun a long time before, back in Saint Ansgar with Mother and Daddy. We weren't big on self-understanding out there in Saint A. But I began to see, too, that I bore more than a little responsibility for the bad behavior visited on me by men, that my relationship to men had been seductive but not acknowledged to be so.

While I was at it, I might as well open my eyes to see that my relations with women had been dishonest, too. Beginning with Mother, they had been tacitly competitive, but also feckless. To be competitive in a healthy and effective way, you have to know what you want, and how to fight for it. I had never learned how to do that. Mother was not a good teacher there. But I was a big girl now, and it was up to me to learn the rules of the game.

There was something bracing about getting this far down to the bitter truth.

I had enjoyed the company I'd kept this day, on this unknown Greek isle, including, for the first time in years, my own. I knew now that I didn't want to be the girl in whose face matches were lit and to whom the pronouncement "First class, absolutely first class" was given. I didn't want to be driven back to my hotel of the moment to spend a quarter hour explaining why I was not making it my driver's hotel of the moment also. I didn't want to be asked to view any sunrises or take any whiskey and sodas with no charge. In short, I did not any longer want to accept others' judgments about me, or about women in general as sex objects.

It was time to step forward and say, *This is me—a wide-eyed child in the body of a woman. Serious, religious, puritanical moralist in horrified transit through the secular, amoral world.*

True, I had found some relief in travel. Moving alone through unfamiliar landscapes, surrounded by strangers speaking a language I didn't understand, was a way of granting myself a parole ticket, of being able to say, *You see, it is quite natural not to understand what people are saying to me, not to know what is expected of me or how I should respond. I am, after all, a person from another country.* In just that way, bolstered fore and aft by comfortable circumlocutions, I had stood, two days earlier, on the deck of the SS *Carina,* bound for Piraeus.

Now, realizing with a start that it was almost four o'clock, I brought my Greek journey to an end.

Changing

I CAME BACK TO MY desk at the magazine in September of '65 ready to undertake the effort of living with a new, more authentic self. It didn't take me long to find out that *The New Yorker*, too, was undergoing significant changes. Back in April, Mr. Shawn's second decade underwent a big shake-up, thanks to the bomblet tossed over the transom by the Talk reporter Constance Feeley's friend Tom Wolfe in the form of a two-part *Herald Tribune* profile of the magazine. "Tiny Mummies! The True Story of the Ruler of 43rd Street's Land of the Walking Dead!" depicted *The New Yorker* as a "mausoleum" and its editor as "the iron mouse." It was, in many ways, a cruel and unfair depiction, but it did have some salutary consequences. Though he said it was a coincidence, Mr. Shawn was prompted to introduce some lively new elements. He hired fresh-minted Harvard hotshots Jake Brackman, Terrence Malick, and Hendrick Hertzberg. He bought a piece by Edward J. Epstein on press mess-ups and herd journalism during the Black Panther coverage. Readers were treated to Ian Frazier casuals about dating his mom. Jamaica Kincaid wrote about her Caribbean childhood, and when Jamaica teamed up with George Trow, the hippest reporter of them all, Talk stories about Roller Derbies began to appear.

Jane Mankiewicz, one of the ever-changing stream of young trainees who did a turn at reception, was emblematic of the new breed. She was a gorgeous young thing, with lustrous black hair down to her shoulders. ("It's Pantene!" she'd say, holding a shiny lock up to the light.) She had the tweed jacket, jeans, and white shirt look down pat. But she was far from vain about her beauty and told me there had been bulimic episodes in her college years when she strove to keep her weight down. I couldn't imagine why, since now she was no more than a size 4. She called herself "a Jewish Princess from Long Island," but that was only one part of her multifaceted and, to me, fascinating life, which included a summer doing voter registration in the Deep South.

Her mother, I learned, was an unabashed supporter of radical causes, and Jane thought it probable that people they knew in these circles had even offered safe houses to Weathermen. I was both admiring and a little scared by all this. Jane delighted in running through the star-studded roster of her paternal lineage: her grandfather Herman, who worked with Orson Welles on *Citizen Kane;* her uncle Joseph, who wrote and directed *All About Eve;* her father, Don, who conceived the television series *Marcus Welby, M.D.* "I *gave* him the Welby part," she told me. "We were kidding around, kicking around the possibilities, you know—Dr. Sawbones, Dr. Getweller, Dr. Bewell. And then it hit me. Dr. *Welby*! I knew right away that was *it.*" A couple of cousins were making their mark, and Jane herself was more than capable of manifesting the family gifts. She wrote and published a poem and a short story that went into the magazine before she left for undetermined pursuits in Florida.

Fresh and freshly enthusiastic while interning at my desk, she gave me a window into the life of the intellectual Left. Never one for half measures, she threw her arms wide and drew me into her circle, and for a while, anyway, in it I was. She introduced me to her boyfriend of the time, a paraplegic writer. Dwayne, as I shall call him, rolled into her apartment, one night when we were all to have dinner together, with a grace and aplomb beyond anything I could have imagined. Jane insisted that her attraction to him had everything to do with his sex appeal. I had made the mistake, when she first told me about the disability, of saying something about its having to be a platonic relationship. "Oh, no," she corrected me, "it's totally sexual. Omigod, that's my main thing." She lapsed into Valley Girl–speak, as she did on occasion when she wished to be especially emphatic.

In the beginning, during Jane's first appearances down on "my" floor, I didn't know what hit me. The first day, I returned from lunch to find the top drawer of my desk cleaned out—not robbed, but set into impeccable order from the jumbled mishmash that was its natural state.

The second day, the books in the corner bookcase were lined up exactly one inch from the edge and arranged in alphabetical order according to author.

The third day, I returned to find that she had been xeroxing her face on the copy machine, with the result that a lurid Jane, with tongue sticking out, was waving from a thumbtack on the bulletin board.

The fourth day, I came back from lunch to find Jane literally wringing her hands. Seeing me, she jumped up and began to wring my hand instead, saying, "You have to find something for me to do. I'm going crazy!"

This absence of assigned activities had never bothered me. I was moving methodically, if slowly, toward a doctorate by taking one course at a time at NYU's Graduate School of Arts and Sciences. So I had long ago perfected the art of serious reading while performing my duties. But Jane was as hyper about reading as about everything else she touched. I understood that something else was going on, that this was not a simple case of boredom induced by idleness. But never having known anyone on amphetamines or other forms of uppers, or simply in a manic state, I was not prepared for anything like the sheer energy that spewed like electrical impulses out of Jane's every pore.

That day she sat me down and said something like this: "Look, in July [it was now early October], my favorite aunt, Josie, was going out for groceries in the Village with her eleven-year-old son, Tim, leaving her nine-year-old son, Nicholas, at home with Peter. That's her husband, Tim and Nick's father, Peter Davis, a filmmaker who was home editing his documentary on Vietnam at the time. You may have seen it—*Hearts and Minds*? It won an Academy Award. Anyway, my aunt Josie stepped off the curb less than a block from her house and was hit by a cab. She never regained consciousness. Josie was like a second mom to me, or maybe more like an older sister. She was seeing me through. I don't know how to understand her death. I can't process it. I need you to be my Josie. You've got to step in here! You're so like her. You even look like her—all wholesome and blond and Waspy while my entire tribe is unmistakably Jewish. You float serene in a world of acceptance while we fight, fight, fight and act like crazy artist mavericks. You *will* step in, won't you? Can I come over to your place for dinner tonight?"

Without waiting for me to answer, Jane went on. "I know a great recipe for chicken. You don't have to do a thing to it but dump in a jar of Smucker's orange marmalade and a package of Lipton's onion soup mix. Then you put it in the oven, and by the time you've had your gin and tonics, it's all done!" I think I nodded weakly at this point. A Smucker's-smothered chicken dinner that night at my house seemed like a done deal.

But Jane was not finished arranging my life. She went on to insist that I spend the rest of the afternoon giving her the lowdown on each of the charges on "my floor."

"You've been here a thousand years. You must know plenty," she speculated. It was seventeen years at that point, but who's counting?

I was not about to tell Jane—or anyone—about the day I found a hooker coming out of one of the writers' offices. Or the day the *Saturday Night Live* crowd (Michael O'Donaghue prominent among their number) came en masse to visit one of the younger Talk reporters. In a short while, the corridor outside that office was filled with wisps of smoke and smelling as sweet as a country meadow.

I did throw Jane a crumb, though, as one of the fact writers went past the reception desk. "See that fellow?" I asked her. "He has absolutely no idea that his wife—also a writer for the magazine—is carrying on with one of the cartoonists down that hall over there."

"Ooh," she cried, clapping her hands, "more, more!"

So I ran down for Jane's benefit the list of evolving relationships that accounted for a string of exchanged editorial females-cum-wives: I told her how Carol Rogge, formerly a secretary in the fiction department, became the second Mrs. Roger Angell; Janet Malcolm, formerly the wife of the theater critic Donald Malcolm, became the second Mrs. Gardner Botsford; Nancy Kraemer, formerly an editorial assistant, became the second Mrs. Whitney Balliett; and Lis

Shabecoff (like Richard Harris's second wife, a member of the magazine's editorial staff) became the third Mrs. Richard Harris. I went on to mention that Kennedy Fraser, who succeeded Lois Long in fashion, became the fourth Mrs. Richard Harris, and that Harris himself, by then in love with somebody else, plunged to his death from a twelfth-story window on the Upper West Side in 1987. While it did not become a case of divorce and remarriage, I told Jane that the double life led by William Shawn and Lillian Ross probably belonged at the head of this list.

Finding that I had dawdled until closing time, I exhaled a discreet sigh of relief as we shut the desk up for the night. Then it was off to Yorkville with Jane in tow.

ONE POSTSCRIPT: the chicken wasn't half-bad.

A Renaissance Man

Some months after my return from Greece, Bernard Taper's wife, Phyllis, recommended the psychoanalyst Daniel Kaplowitz to me and got me into treatment. Kaplowitz had been trained in eclectic therapy of the Erik Erikson type. In addition to his private practice, he served in high office at one of the New York psychoanalytic associations. A tall, ruggedly handsome man, with a basketball player's height and physique (he was an All-American guard in college at Long Island University), he combined eminence in his field with domestic happiness. In his forties, he shared with his patients—or at least with me—occasional glimpses of a solid second marriage with his wife, herself a professional woman, and their baby son.

I saw him through the rosy light of positive transference, of course, but I didn't make it up that he played Bach partitas on the violin between patients. He was my idea of a Renaissance man. I was to see him three times a week for fifty-minute sessions on the couch and once a week for sessions of group therapy for the next ten years. He diagnosed my illness as passive dependency and said, after our initial consultation, "I have a dream for you, Janet. I see us working productively together to get to the bottom of some of these problems that have been troubling you, until you walk out of here one day, a lovely woman, well at ease." I don't know about the "lovely" part, but he delivered on the rest big-time, and I was enchanted by his reference to Chaucer's Criseyde: "I am mine own woman, well at ease."

It took ten years of work together, but he helped me weave into an integrated self the frayed threads of my troubled childhood in Iowa and the body of experience I found so hard to assimilate in New York. He began by encouraging me to tell it my way, in my own good time. I described a young woman who was not a genius, but who was of better than average intelligence, for whom life was mainly experienced as a snarl of impressions and memories. Like Joyce's Stephen Dedalus in female guise, I moved through the streets of New York, sifting and weighing and organizing the new sensations that were coming swiftly at me from all directions, then attempting to make sense of them. A task as daunting as the creation of a world. The good doctor helped me to see that a number of aspects of my disintegrated self complicated this attempt. They operated like a series of filters between me and my experiences.

One was my shame over my origins in Iowa. Imagine feeling inferiority over a landscape when one has been surrounded in childhood by the richest farmland in the world. Still, measured against the twisted trees and mountain crags of Arthur Rackham's illustrations in my children's books, the Disney forests and castles of *Snow White,* the skyscrapers of Manhattan, or the Nevadan deserts and Colorado Rockies of the movies I saw—my only points of geographic reference—northern Iowa looked flat and inferior. But more shameful than that was the position I and my family occupied in our small town. This was a puzzling mix of better housing but worse moral standing than the families of my cousins and peers. The mohair sofa and the black upright piano didn't glean me anything but an occasional accusation of snootiness—and I was, from my earliest appearance on the scene, a hypersensitive social barometer of the impression I was making on those around me. Even harder to bear were the expressions of gleeful pity—the schadenfreude—flitting across the faces of the adults, and the children who mimicked them, over the sight of Father reeling from drink or Mother pretending he was not. I told Dr. Kaplowitz of my preschool habit of crawling under the counter in our family grocery. I could still see myself cowering in the space between the wrapping paper and the string, beneath the cash register. I remembered being perfectly able to see through the three-inch wood and veneer of the countertop to read those faces of public scorn.

Another locus of shame was my unworthy self-image—a gift, unconsciously bestowed, from that loving mother who was a vain, pretty, Irene Dunne look-alike. I believed that she competed with me, her little blond daughter, for Father's love. Not the reeling, drunken father, but the dashing, charming father, better with people than even she was, because more authentic. Not pretty enough. Not graceful enough. Not nice enough. Just not *enough* to be able to hope for his love. Or that of the boys. Or the men. My insecurity, confusion, conflict, and paralysis of will in dealing with the world was the area Dr. Kaplowitz zeroed in on as the territory we had to work through. The way it seems to me now, I was always, somewhere deep in my healthy core, a bright, perceptive, sensitive, observant, loving, and lovable human being. The painfully shy, vain, self-centered, insecure, and rather hateful little girl who grew into me as a teenager and then a young woman was forever masquerading as the former, while in touch only with the hated monster who was always, I was sure, threatened with exposure. Dan Kaplowitz and I worked hard to get those fragmented pieces to coalesce.

Then there was the shame of the writer who doesn't write. The me who carried within my breast in equal shares the conviction that I could write and the certainty that I could not. Here all the problems of shame over childhood inadequacy and adult insecurity and sexual insecurity and social insecurity ganged up to produce periodic bouts of thwarted attempts. I told Dr. Kaplowitz about the pile of half-filled blue composition books that trailed behind me every place I lived. At this point, Dr. K. deftly turned the table on me. He asked me why, after earning my master's from NYU in 1968, I was not working toward a doctorate, though he knew what my answer would be—I feared the daunting task of writing a dissertation. When I gave him the answer anyway, he said, "That's not being a very good sport, is it?" Which I accepted as the prescription for self-respect that it was.

"You mean," I asked, "you think I could get a PhD?"

We were standing at his door at the end of a session, always a protean moment. He smiled and said, "Isn't it about time you did something that was *good* for you?" His suggestion turned out well. I began to substitute for the blue notebooks a second pile of academic accomplishments that I knew to be within my grasp. Thirty years of teaching and five volumes on Edmund Wilson stand as something of a tribute to his lucky hit.

We didn't get everything sorted out in our work together. Even now there are days, just after some rejection or disappointment in my private or professional pursuits, when it feels as if I shall have to begin all over again. But I emerged with a better, more generous acceptance of my Iowa childhood, a clear acknowledgment of my parents' *Menschlichkeit*—that good word that seems to get at the idea of humanness better than the English word *humanity*—and, it could be, the beginnings of my own.

Mr. Right at Last

Albert Aaron Lazar first appeared in my life as the evil one, took on physical form as my landlord, and eventually became my husband. Al, owner of the building that housed the cartoonist Evan Simm's studio on West Fourth Street (the scene of my biblical seduction), was a Pittsburgh-born entrepreneur with multiple interests, among them the manufacture of raffia shoes. He was Evan's role model for moving through the Village scene with utmost cool, leaving women strewn in his wake, a wife among them. In his early fifties then, Al was tall, trim, a look-alike of Walter Pidgeon, with Pidgeon's deep voice, cultured, but a touch gruff. (He once admitted to me that he was kind of pleased when, crossing on the *France* in the late 1940s, word circled the ship that he *was* Walter Pidgeon, on his way to California to make a picture with Merle Oberon.)

Al Lazar liked art. Although he barely drank, he was a familiar figure in the Cedar Tavern, where he hung out with the action painters Franz Kline, Willem de Kooning, and Jackson Pollock. He liked artists of all kinds, writers, painters, actors, and even charlatans. He would buy interesting old buildings in the West Village and rent them at ruinously small sums to such creative types. He preferred it to opening the doors of his charming brownstones to run-of-the mill tenants who might be better business risks.

Evan admired the man's savoir faire, his air of self-possession, which cut such a wide swath with the ladies. People said that Al was not quite divorced from the millionaire wife who waited with the kids in a Connecticut exurb to bask in his rare presence. That only increased his stature in Evan's eyes. He was, in any event, a fixture at the swingingest parties of the sixties. If Ornette Coleman bought an abandoned schoolhouse on the Lower East Side and threw himself a birthday party, Al was there. If the de Koonings and their fellow pioneers in abstract expressionism opened a loft with a keg and a couple of lines in the adjacent john, Al was there. If Andy Warhol and Andy's girls were at a party come some September night on Watts or Delancey, Al was there—and Andy's Goth chick, Viva, went home with him. All in all, Al had the mojo Evan craved, and he spoke of him to me in the reverent tones of a hero worshipper. I was royally turned off on all counts—womanizer, wife betrayer, child deserter, partygoer, Viva boinker—and I was having none of it.

By the time I was sold on renting an apartment from Al, on the third-floor rear of his building on West Twelfth, I had such a low opinion of him that I refused to sign the lease unless there was an attorney present. This broke him up—the transaction involved all of eighty dollars a month, utilities included. We met in 1960, and it would be a good decade before he was more than my landlord. Many years later, Al told me he fell in love with me when I walked into his lawyer's office on my lunch hour. (It was handily located on Forty-Second Street, just around the corner from *The New Yorker*.) I was wearing black heels, a black-and-white houndstooth coatdress, a black beret, and short white cotton gloves. "I was thunderstruck," he said. But if he was wooing me then, or in the years that followed, he was so subtle I didn't know it. He would come by and sit in my narrow sunporch, having a cup of coffee and passing the time of day. He asked a great many questions about where I came from and how I liked it there and how I liked it here, but I thought he was just being a very nice landlord.

One by one, all of Evan's bad knocks against Al got erased by the facts or, if not erased, certainly mitigated. He did not abandon a wife; they'd divorced several years earlier. He did not desert his children; they were in his apartment weekly and on his lips always (for they were bright boys, and their accomplishments were many). He did admit to seeing a zonked-out Viva home one night, but he was so full of compassion for her as a lost person, it didn't seem to qualify as exploitation of women. In 1964, when I was still grieving over the loss of Fritz, Al lent me his house on the Vineyard for a week to salve my broken heart. The next year, when I expressed the desire to go into retreat, he lent me his A-frame in Connecticut for a month, dropping off what he dubbed a housewarming bottle of champagne. By the time I returned from Oxford in 1966, he was calling now and then with tickets to the opera or a Mozart concert or a suggestion that Nina Simone was at the Vanguard and he was pretty sure I'd like her. When he found out I'd never seen a horse race, he piled me into his 1964 red Mustang and off we went to Belmont Park.

The irony was that in 1970, just when I began to realize he was much more to me than a nice landlord, Al said we'd probably better not see each other anymore. He knew that I wanted to marry and have children. I should do that. I'd be good at it. He just had to be truthful and say he'd been there and done that. So I took myself off to a new apartment in Yorkville, and it was 1975, the year my father died (*pace* Freud), before I saw him again.

Ever obliging, I spent the interval looking for Mr. Right. My new buddies at Saint Peter's Lutheran were most attentive. I saw shows, went to dinner, stayed out of bed, and in general behaved myself. There was a biologist, a stockbroker, an ad man, and a minister who came and went without incident. Oddly, there was another German, too. Kurt was a divorced political science professor who taught at a large nearby university and was looking for a stepmother for his seven-year-old son, the apple of his eye. (I have changed his name and that of his son here.) The boy's mother was carrying on a passionate affair with the man of the hour in left-wing circles, one of those beating the drum for a War on Poverty. But the little boy was not getting the attention his father thought he deserved. After several weeks of wining and dining me and making me a gift of the complete Mozart symphonies—with Leinsdorf conducting—Kurt asked me to come up to his ex-wife's house on the New England shore. It was right on the water, and he thought we could try out our fit as a family. But it was a disaster. The little boy, accustomed to entering his dad's bedroom whenever he wakened in the middle of the night, did so and discovered the beast with two backs. Kurt was horrified. He made me remove myself to the guest bedroom immediately, while little Christopher was taken into the paternal arms for comfort. Even if there had been no such mischance, however, I had the sense to see it was a no-go.

When I came back from my father's funeral in 1975 and was

moping around with no future husband in sight, Al called to say that he'd seen my review of Edmund Wilson's *The Twenties* in the Catholic intellectual periodical *Commonweal.* He'd been going through some of the magazines and journals in the Vineyard Haven Public Library, and there I was! He'd read it and liked what I wrote. He'd just come down to the city for the rest of the winter. Was I, by any chance, free for dinner? I was. With twice the twelve years between us my parents had boasted, we two had all the makings of a classic May-December love. I have always had a weakness for "September Song"—and so it came about that after many a year searching and not finding, at the age of thirty-nine, in a man old enough to be my father, I finally found a guy I could trust. He was all the hard-to-find qualities I'd sought for combined. Knowing how rare a combination it was, I was loath to let a little thing like one score and four stand in my way. The elusive traits? Sober, sexy, self-assured, sensitive, and—to get out of the *s*'s—brilliant, his own man, capable of independent thought, no slave to capitalism or orthodoxy or any of the structures he was born into, making a place for himself in the world that he could comfortably be himself in. All that, and he loved opera, too.

When Al said anything, he conveyed the sense that his words were coming from a man who had earned them. The list of constraints on his freedom was the list of things he had successfully broken from, beginning with his Orthodox father's expectation that his first and only identity was to be a good Jew. By the time I met him, Al was thoroughly assimilated. He told me he had spent the better part of his youth divesting himself—"freeing" himself, as he put it—of that identity, not from blasphemous rejection of its tenets or in loathing recoil from its burdensome stereotypes, but as a necessary precondition for finding himself. That done, he wore the badge lightly, often citing the British neurosurgeon–artistic director Jonathan Miller's answer to the "What religion are you?" line on his army questionnaire. In Al's telling, it was "I'm not a Jew—but I am Jew-ish."

Free of his father, Al spent the next forty years rejecting the other external pressures he'd felt, to be a certain way, look or sound a certain way, conform to a certain set of rules or expectations. He had made his way through Harvard College and found that his love of literature did not reconcile him to the prospect of life in the ivory tower. Upon finishing Harvard Law School, he felt a similar reluctance to enter a life spent practicing law. In the end, he left the academic halls with the spirit of Thoreau at the core of his being. He became a sayer of no.

Al had seen brutal things in the war, which contributed to his strength. When I gave him my trust, I relied not just on what I knew of Al's having earned the right to his self-knowledge but on what I knew of his regard for women. He wasn't flashy about it. He just went out of his way to treat me and every woman he met with his full interest and attention. On the matter of the battle of the sexes, it was rich how one-sided our setup was. Al walked away with the win before I even took the field. His preemptive strike was twofold.

When we began to spend time exclusively with each other—in the summer of 1976—he said apropos of nothing one day, "No talk about 'relationships,' understood?" I think I did have the presence of mind to ask, "Why?"

"It's a waste of time," he said. "The existentialists have it right.

Whatever is the case, is. No amount of talk is going to change it. The only thing we have to feel responsible for to each other is to pay attention to what's happening between us. It either is or it isn't."

So be it, I thought. Like all of Al's life rules, it sounded a lot easier than it was.

Still, there was one transcendent morning in the house on the Vineyard that I would not trade for all the relationship talk in the world. It was early morning, and after making love in Al's old maple bed, we lay, not talking, in each other's arms. I could hear the leaves rustle in the window just above our heads. The morning sun sent a golden shaft across us from the east. I had the strong sensation of being in a tough, lacelike, open net, suspended over the void. Utterly at risk, yet utterly secure. It was a new sensation for me. *This,* I thought, *is what it feels like to feel loved.* Like Dickens's Little Dorrit, I had been unable to believe I could be. Now, with no declarations of any kind on his part, and knowing there would be none, with Al, I believed.

Later that day we were lying on the beach, and the second of Al's rules to live by came down. Al, as usual, in the altogether, and me in my yellow two-piece. He was on a large bath sheet, and I on my favorite beach towel, a long rectangle of royal blue with a border of melon, lemon, navy, and chartreuse. The Red Sox were ahead of the Yankees, six–zip, in the bottom of the ninth—this was good because we were Red Sox fans, Al since his Harvard days, and I since being with Al—when he reached over and turned the game off.

"If we're going to be going on as we seem to be, I need to make a few things clear about what you should expect. I guess I mean what you should not expect," he said. He was trying to sound offhand, but I know an important moment when I hear one. I was all ears.

"The biggest thing," he went on, "is that I will never do anything to please you. I mean, I don't expect or want to do anything to displease you. But I will never do anything at all just because you want me to do it."

I was stunned as I tried to hold on to the huge difference that had just opened up between us. I was, every minute we were together, bending every fiber of my being into the shape or response that I thought would please him. It now occurred to me with blinding clarity that I had been doing that with every man I'd known from the moment I'd lain in Daddy's arms and he'd read to me about "Bye, Baby Bunting" in the big double bed in Saint Ansgar.

How was this to be? Not to live to please the man? Whom, then, to please? Something I had, on occasion, felt stirring in me in Dr. Kaplowitz's office was given a new lease on life that day. The idea of an autonomous me. It was in 1976, toward the end of our work together, that I lay on the couch in Dan Kaplowitz's office and said, "Al says, 'Women are just as good as men,' and then he says, 'And it's not men's fault that women don't know that.' How do you like them apples?" The good doctor did not hesitate: "Hold on to that guy," he said.

Here I am reminded of Dr. Kaplowitz's assessment as we parted. It was my last appointment before leaving New York. "You have made a lot of progress," he said. "You have worked hard. I think you have largely resolved your conflicts with your father. Probably allowing Al into your life has helped you with that. As my old mentor at the Menninger Clinic used to say, 'We are all of us searching for a perfect family. Sometimes we substitute material things, but often in the friendships we form, the lovers we take, the mates we marry, we are arranging for ourselves the understanding mother, the good father, the loving brother and sister we yearn for, the things we missed in our own.'"

Learning to listen to the inner me and to respond with emotional honesty was only one of the things Al taught me. He also gave me new perspective on what I thought of as my problems. I remember coming back from dinner at the old Jaeger House in Yorkville one spring night. We were crossing Eighty-Fifth Street and threading our way through puddles after a heavy rain. I had been holding forth on the subject of the stereotype I felt trapped and belittled and stymied me, the perception of me as a dumb blond.

"You don't know what real stereotypes are," Al said in that blunt, authoritative voice that carried all the weight in the world. "Negroes or blacks or African Americans by whatever name are still trapped in the racial stereotypes that date back to the eighteenth century at least. Maybe even to biblical times." He paused to help me jump a puddle. "You should have been born a Jew. Or black, or something with real hardship attached to it. As it is, you just—I'm sorry if it sounds unsympathetic—but you just don't know what you're talking about."

I think one of the reasons Al could say these blunt things without offense was the self-deprecating humor he practiced. He'd listen to the outcome of an election he'd predicted would be won by the man or woman who lost, the ball game he'd placed a bad bet on, the real estate deal that fell through, and say, "Wrong again." There was a definite dark streak to his sense of comedy that reminded me of Joe

Mitchell. Al loved to tell a variation of the old law-school poser he heard from Bill de Kooning. "Bill's version has the guy jumping off a twenty-story building to commit suicide. As he passes the tenth floor, a wag in the open window shouts, 'How's it going?' And the guy answers, 'So far, so good.'" Al always laughed when he told that one.

Watching Al on the tennis courts—staying on the back court, placing his shots, and running his younger opponents ragged—taught me all I didn't know and, not having played sports, had never learned about the way to compete gracefully in the world. "Girls don't play sports," my mother said, writing a health excuse for me to skip gym. "Boys play sports. That's the way it should be." But she didn't practice what she preached. Mother's competition of choice was in the field of games, not sports, but there she was a wicked competitor. A demon cardplayer, she excelled at whist and contract bridge (Goren rules) and, in her eighties, regularly outfoxed her neighbors in the assisted-living complex by tracking and accessing the best cards on bingo night. I never learned any games, at the card table or on the athletic field. I never learned the most common sports, like swimming or bicycle riding. Those things were not important for girls, especially smart career girls like me. So spoke my mother out of her lying mouth.

Al, however, made the point again and again. He himself played on the town courts in Vineyard Haven, swam daily from July to October, and followed professional tennis, baseball, basketball, and football on TV. He was full of sage responses as he watched individual plays. "It's a mental game, always," he'd say, "even beyond the willingness to practice your ass off. It's a matter of confidence. That's what I try, more than anything else, to give my boys. The athlete or the team—or the horse and jockey—that has it is the one with the competitive edge." For most of my life, until I worked with Dr. K. and knew Al, what I lacked most and tried to learn from them was confidence.

Because it was a way of speaking that he detested, my darling Al refused to, as he put it, "talk about relationships." Yet the only terms he would accept in our relating to one another were, I now see, precisely those of Buber's I-Thou. Whenever I would lay down a distance of withdrawal from him, he pointed it out to me and called me back. I love him for many things, but most of all I love him for that.

MY BRIEF PERIOD OF sexual acting out brought me closer than I'd ever been to the hopelessness that verges on despair. Perhaps that is why tawdry seduction scenes have become emblematic for me of nothingness—the void devoid of meaning that I call the yawning abyss. Sometimes in the bad old days, when I and one of my Daddy substitutes were sitting in a bar somewhere, working our way through the tired old scenario of seduction as if it were brand new and its outcome still a mystery, I would flash on the deep pit opening before me—the world without meaning, without hope. Then some sharp ching of silverware against glass, or the clatter of dishes from the kitchen as a waiter passed through the swinging door, would bring me back to the moment. But the knowledge of that abyss was always with me. It always is with anyone who has been there. I am aware of that. No shortage in this world of despair, and no pretending that mine was preceded by any great shakes as far as human suffering goes. But one thing I *have* learned is to see it as a piece of the larger truth, the tragic view of the world all enlightened folk from Aristotle and Christ to Shakespeare and Chekhov and Joan Didion and Philip Roth have seen, and to respect it.

What the Receptionist Received

In 1976 *The New Yorker* underwent a period of inner strife as Mr. Shawn struggled with an employee rebellion and a bid from the Newspaper Guild to unionize. Without moving a muscle I became a bone of contention. I was both held up as the poster child for gender discrimination and reviled as an Uncle Tom.

If my twenty-one years there is to have any clarity, I will have to confront those disparate views, beginning with the question, why did the magazine never find a better job for me?

As far as I know, with the exception of the brief mismatch of me and the art department, I was never seriously considered for promotion to any other job or floor. Oh, once, in 1964 or so, Dorothy Morrison from Goings On About Town came down to ask me if I thought I would be happy checking movie schedules and theater openings from a two-person office tucked away in the back corridors of the nineteenth floor. When I said I was afraid I would find it repetitive and isolated, she agreed and said I'd made the right choice turning it down.

In 1965 I asked Lou Forster to consider me for a fact-checking job. He said that I was too pretty to bury my light under that bushel—that I should probably consider modeling. In 1975, when I had begun to publish book reviews in *Commonweal,* I asked Edith Oliver to consider me for reviewer in the Briefly Noted section of the books department. She said the Briefly Noted slots were entirely filled by writers already under contract.

In 1976, when I was finishing my course work toward a PhD in twentieth-century British and American literature at NYU and beginning work on my dissertation subject, the *New Yorker* writer Edmund Wilson, I asked Roger Angell, who was head of the fiction department, to consider me as a first reader. He said I was disqualified for the job by my overfamiliarity with the type of fiction *The New Yorker* had been publishing in the nineteen years I'd been there. He said they were through being constricted by a reputation for buying and printing only "*New Yorker* type" short stories. They wanted a fresh eye and a multilinguist, ready to find authors from places like Lithuania, and I would be all wrong for that.

For some time I was tempted to regard my failure to advance as a reflection of nepotism at the top. Roger Angell, for example, was the son of the fiction editor Katharine S. White and the stepson of E. B. White. The senior editor Gardner Botsford was the stepson of one of the owners of the magazine. The Talk reporter Susan Lardner was the granddaughter of Ring. The head of maintenance, John O'Brian, was the nephew of the office manager, Sheila McGrath. Renata Adler was engaged to Edmund Wilson's son Reuel, Janet Malcolm was the wife of the theater critic Donald Malcolm, and so on. If the family member was not directly associated with the magazine, a famous relative turned up with disconcerting regularity on the editorial rolls: Leonard Bernstein's brother, Burton; William Murray, the son of Janet Flanner's inamorata Natalia Murray; Henry Cooper, the great-great-grandnephew of James Fenimore Cooper;

and Tony Hiss, the son of Alger Hiss, all worked at the magazine for varying periods of time. Less a matter of bloodlines but equally compelling were the ties that bound certain figures on the editorial roster to certain eastern Ivy campuses. Calvin Trillin, Henry Cooper, and Gerald Jonas were the Yalies; Ved Mehta, George Trow, Tony Hiss, Bill Wertenbaker, and Rick Hertzberg were the Harvard boys. Not that I was keeping track!

But of course the nepotism and Ivy League theories break down when one takes into account the many others who had left their trainee status at my desk and gone on to become contributors. They had done so by the simple expedient of submitting—and having had published—poetry, Talk stories, and short fiction.

What of my manuscripts? What of my submissions? Few. Few, and far between. I believe the sum total of my submissions in those twenty-one years was three: A poem, which reaped for me a sweet personal rejection note, promptly sent by Howard Moss, who certainly had not fashioned it to discourage me from submitting more. A caption for the end-of-column typos called newsbreaks, which was likewise rejected kindly and in short order by Burt Bernstein, who took over that department when Mr. White announced he'd done it long enough.

Last was a Talk story of a timely nature, which I submitted to Mr. Shawn. When weeks went by and I heard nothing, I contacted Mr. Shawn's secretary, Mary Painter, who got back to me rather sheepishly later that day and said that unfortunately my manuscript had been lost on the bottom of a pile of papers on his desk and was, in any case, no longer timely. I have to say I did resent that a little.

Still, there was no getting around the facts: My paltry offerings flew in the face of plain evidence all around me that such submissions—far more frequent and focused on creative work—would be vital to realizing my dream. And vital to the question of why I stayed at *The New Yorker* for twenty-one years and never wrote a word for it.

But was there a reason the magazine never found a better job for me?

Perhaps I do have the answer after all. I had it when my Talk story got lost, when a falsehood was told me about no openings in book reviewing, and when I was cut out of a job as first reader by a trumped-up story about Eastern European fiction. By then I had long since come to realize—or should have—that mothering, nurturing, providing a discreet and loyal personification of continuity on the writer's floor, was exactly the position in which the editors wanted me or indeed felt they had any use for me.

Did that make me a victim? Or a beneficiary? It seems to me a two-way street. When the Newspaper Guild reps looked at my salary record ($80 a week to start and $163 to finish), they were incensed, and much was said about the way the magazine was exploiting me. However, as I look back on the eight trips to Europe the magazine underwrote (by way of lengthy vacations in the summers, two of which stretched to eight weeks away or more, four of them with pay); my twelve years of graduate school; ten years of expensive psychoanalysis with a top Manhattan analyst (if the magazine chose to exploit my passive dependency, they paid handsomely to rid me of it); coverage of my desk to permit a Thursday-Friday trip up to Poughkeepsie to teach a course at Vassar; as well as the many intangibles that came to me in the way of invitations to share the cultural, social, and literary life of the city and, by extension, the wider world, it is not clear to me who was exploiting whom.

One very attractive aspect of the union movement for me was its emphasis on solidarity. I loved the discussions held over wine and cheese with just *New Yorker* people present as we met in off-site locations to hash out the pros and cons of joining the Newspaper Guild. John Bennet led the first of these—I think it was in Dan Menaker's West Side apartment. Nat Hentoff, the jazz columnist for many years on *The Village Voice,* sat in as an advocate in the meeting Ruth Rogin held at her place downtown.

Full of community spirit, I, too, held one of the early meetings at my place in Yorkville. It was before the editors and drawing-account writers were exempted—they were defined as belonging to management, which must have dismayed them. So all the checkers and Fred Shapiro (ex-newspaperman and strong critic of the Guild) and a number of the writers and editors were there. At that meeting I realized that the existential angst I once allowed to trouble me—was I or was I not "one of them?"—had faded into nothingness. That night there was a palpable feeling of solidarity in the air and I was never more certain I belonged.

Ultimately, the attempt to unionize *The New Yorker* was voted down. An in-house bargaining unit was formed. Quite apart from any formal bargain, the magazine and I arrived at our own peace. With the full support of editorial management, I made plans to move on. Everything I needed to complete the work toward my doctorate—paid leave, time off, early departure to make class—was cheerfully granted. All of which left me, one spring a couple of years later, with a job to go to at the University of Cincinnati and a dissertation on Edmund Wilson under way.

It was only natural, of course, that my feelings about leaving the magazine after so many years should be mixed. On the plus side I had a much firmer grasp on my identity. I was no longer dependent upon the *New Yorker* mantle of borrowed fame to find a sense of my own worth. My analysis, my doctorate, and my conquest of Al were much healthier sources of self-respect (though I was not immune to feeling some ego gratification at walking off with an alpha male like Al). And certainly I had no question that it was time—I was more than ready to move onward and upward. But the thought of separation was also bittersweet. In the end, I had to leave the safety of that long-familiar cocoon to find the self I'd sought on that turnaround trip to Greece.

In May 1978, when word got around that the next Friday would be my last day on the reception desk, somebody—I don't know who, but it was sure to have been one of the women—organized a farewell of sorts. Too informal to be called a party, it was typical of the kind of gesture that accompanied birthdays or leave-takings at the magazine. It was held at about four o'clock in the lounge by the back stairs. People came out of their offices and ate a slice of "Good Luck, Jan!" cake off paper plates and drank champagne from plastic flutes. Then Mr. Shawn came down, which wasn't typical. Someone handed him a single red rose, which he presented to me.

I SUPPOSE YOU COULD say it was the end of an era.

Acknowledgments

In the writing of any book the author racks up debts of gratitude for help of one kind or another, and my case is no exception. First and foremost is the debt I owe to my late, brilliant collaborator on three Edmund Wilson books, David Castronovo. During the ten enjoyable years we put our heads together over Wilson, David's surgical wit, his gift for brevity, and his example made me a better writer. He loved this book. His last gift to me was the devoted circle of his admirers, who, led by his sister Val and her family, have rallied around it too.

Among *New Yorker* writers, past and present, who saw early chapters and lent valuable comment and support were Henry Cooper, Gerry Jonas, Wally White, Lis Harris, Anthony Bailey, and Calvin Trillin. Family members and friends were generous in their praise and helpful in getting the facts right, especially my brother and his wife, Joe and Nancy Groth, and two cousins, Karen Steinberg and Doreen Finnesgaard. Special thanks for guidance on early drafts to Elizabeth Guyer Ebel, Ivy Bannister, Margaret Tully, Jalana Lazar, Corey Lazar, Annie-B Parson, Gene Gill, Mary Rose Main, Mary McNamara, Leslie Davis, Theasa Tuohy, Susannah and Mac Talley, Gretchen Shine, Liz Bowman, Marcia Schlaff, Ann Tracy, Elsa Solender, and Yasuko Hatano-Collier.

My agent Carolyn Larson gave me unwavering support and the invaluable gift of placing the manuscript with Amy Gash, senior editor par excellence at Algonquin Books. In her nurturing hands it has grown from its initial embryonic shape into the full-fledged *Receptionist* you see before you. The midwife who gave our new delivery a life-giving pat on the back was Elisabeth Scharlatt, Algonquin's publisher. To the art, production, and promotion departments, especially the designer of the jacket and Megan Fishmann, I owe the attractive packaging and the promotional boost that sends her forth looking her best. My thanks to all.

The Receptionist

A Conversation with Janet Groth

Questions for Discussion

A Conversation with Janet Groth

What do you think accounts for our fascination with this period in history, and also our fascination with The New Yorker*?*

So much change was taking place in America in the era of rock 'n' roll, the sexual and social revolutions represented by feminism and the civil rights movement—we just can't get enough of digging around in it to figure how we got to where we are now. Partly I think our fascination with *The New Yorker* stems from its continuity. While everything else changed around it, the magazine kept on coming out, week after week, with pretty much the same format, recording the times and events swirling around it with reassuringly steady and trenchant voices. The cartoons gave amusing form to our dismay, the editorial content could be relied upon to attempt analysis of its causes, and even the ads assured us we could—or somebody could—buy things that would effectively mask it.

How did you decide what to include and what to leave out as you took us on your journey of self-discovery?

Once I committed fully to doing it, I exercised no censorship at all. Ultimately it was my editor who made a few judicious suggestions for cutting—all in the direction of excising what the kids nowadays call "TMI."

How long did it take you to write The Receptionist*?*

I sometimes answer this question—it comes up a lot—by saying that it took the whole of my adult life. But, if you mean the time between my first serious probe of all the little blue notebooks I kept while working at the magazine and when I submitted the manuscript for publication, the answer is five years.

What did you learn during the period covered in the book, when you were around great writers, that you have taken into your own writing?

I discovered and lived the bleak truth behind Joyce's line "I bleed by the black stream for my torn bow!"—which to me means that art is the result of wresting part of the artist's very being from within. (Wilson used those words as the epigram for *The Wound and the Bow.*) From the thirty-two-year writer's block of essayist Joseph Mitchell—and from my own long artistic silence—I learned that the shadow of potential failure accompanies each attempt to put words on paper. From critic Dwight Macdonald I learned a guiding principle of structural organization—"Put everything you have to say about one thing in the same place." And, from E. B. White, who interviewed me for my position at the magazine, I learned via his classic *Elements of Style* to construct most sentences with a subject, a verb, and a predicate, in that order.

Tell me about your research. Did you do much fact-checking, or did you rely primarily on memory?

I did a surprising amount of research, considering that my material was ostensibly residing in my own memory. I had, in addition to those notebooks, every telephone message, every drawing or scrap of paper or photograph, to which I refer in the pages of my book. I double-checked dates and places. I often turned to the *Complete New Yorker* on disc. That was enormously helpful. Then I discovered there are still proofreaders, text editors, and page proof readers who work on facts as well as grammar and syntax. Algonquin staff were always asking me to correct, approve, or verify suggested changes at every stage of production. This was also much to my surprise, since I had had it told to me often, by writers publishing with other houses, that such meticulous editorial attention to detail was a thing of the past.

What challenges did writing this book pose, and how did you overcome them?

Much of the way around the hardest obstacles was won by hard work on the analyst's couch. Learning to confront one's self is number one on the memoirist's list of tasks, and that one I had, finally, learned how to do. Then it was a question of deciding which identities I needed to protect, if not for the subjects' sake, for the sake of their offspring.

Did the manuscript change much during the editing process?

As the sitcom writers are fond of saying, "Don't get me started!" My editor was, and is, my guardian angel, overseeing every moment of the transformation between the typescript I originally submitted and the book now on bookstore shelves—and readers' shelves—as

The Receptionist. She saw the story of my failure to advance as key to the arc of the book and gave it, right from the start of our work together, not only its coherent shape but its title! We moved a chapter from the very back of the manuscript, where I had buried it, to the front. Several all-day sessions—working from first page to last—resulted in the loss of some material, and a few pages, not to do with that arc, were sacrificed, but we came out with the story you now see. I am most grateful.

What advice do you have for first-time memoirists about writing?

Get thee to thy computers, potential writers. And, if blocked, get thee to a good analyst!

What advice do you have for first-time memoirists about breaking into publishing?

There I think the best advice I can give is to do some book reviewing. It was my way into print, and it is still a good way.

Are you currently working on another book?

Always, as is, I suspect, every writer. There is always some new material incubating just under the surface of the conscious brain. But, beyond saying that I am fielding requests for my story to be continued, that's all I'll say just now.

Adapted from an interview conducted by Ellen Birkett Morris with Janet Groth published on Authorlink (authorlink.com).

Questions for Discussion

1. The journey from small town to big city to seek one's fortune is one that women—and men—have been making for a long time. How did the author's midcentury trajectory differ from the journey a young woman might make today? How are the hurdles she faced the same or different from those women of the twenty-first century face?

2. Do you think the author's inability to advance at *The New Yorker* was due to her own insecurities, or was she a victim of the era's workplace biases against women? Was she a victim more of time and circumstance or of her own limitations?

3. Are there other classic coming-of-age stories—fiction or nonfiction—to which you would compare the author's tale?

4. The author befriended some of the country's greatest writers and harbored her own dreams of writing. Yet she didn't publish any of her own work until decades later. How do you think those close relationships informed her own creative endeavors—or lack thereof?

5. Were you familiar with the writers discussed in the book? If so, did the book add to your understanding and appreciation of them? If not, did the book lead you to want to read their work?

6. How did the author's suicide attempt, her period of promiscuity, and her opening of her home to an African American roommate contribute to her understanding of herself and of the wider world?

7. Did the mores of the men in this book seem different from those of single men today?

8. At one point Al tells the author, "Women are just as good as men. . . . And it's not men's fault that women don't know that" (page 219). What do you think about that comment?

9. Do you see the author growing into what her analyst said she could become: "A lovely woman, well at ease" (page 208)?

10. At the end of the book the author wonders whether *The New Yorker* took advantage of her or whether she took advantage of the magazine. Which do you think?

SUSANNAH TALLEY

Janet Groth, Emeritus Professor of English at the State University of New York at Plattsburgh, has also taught at Vassar, Brooklyn College, the University of Cincinnati, and Columbia. She was a Fulbright lecturer in Norway and a visiting fellow at Yale and is the author of *Edmund Wilson: A Critic for Our Time* (for which she won the NEMLA Book Award) and coauthor with David Castronovo of *Critic in Love: A Romantic Biography of Edmund Wilson.* She lives in New York City.

Join us at **AlgonquinBooksBlog.com** for the latest news on all of our stellar titles, including weekly giveaways, behind-the-scenes snapshots, book and author updates, original videos, media praise, detailed tour information, and other exclusive material.
You'll also find information about the **Algonquin Book Club**, a selection of the perfect books—from award winners to international bestsellers—to stimulate engaging and lively discussion. Helpful book group materials are available, including

Book excerpts
Downloadable discussion guides
Author interviews
Original author essays
Book club tips and ideas
Wine pairings